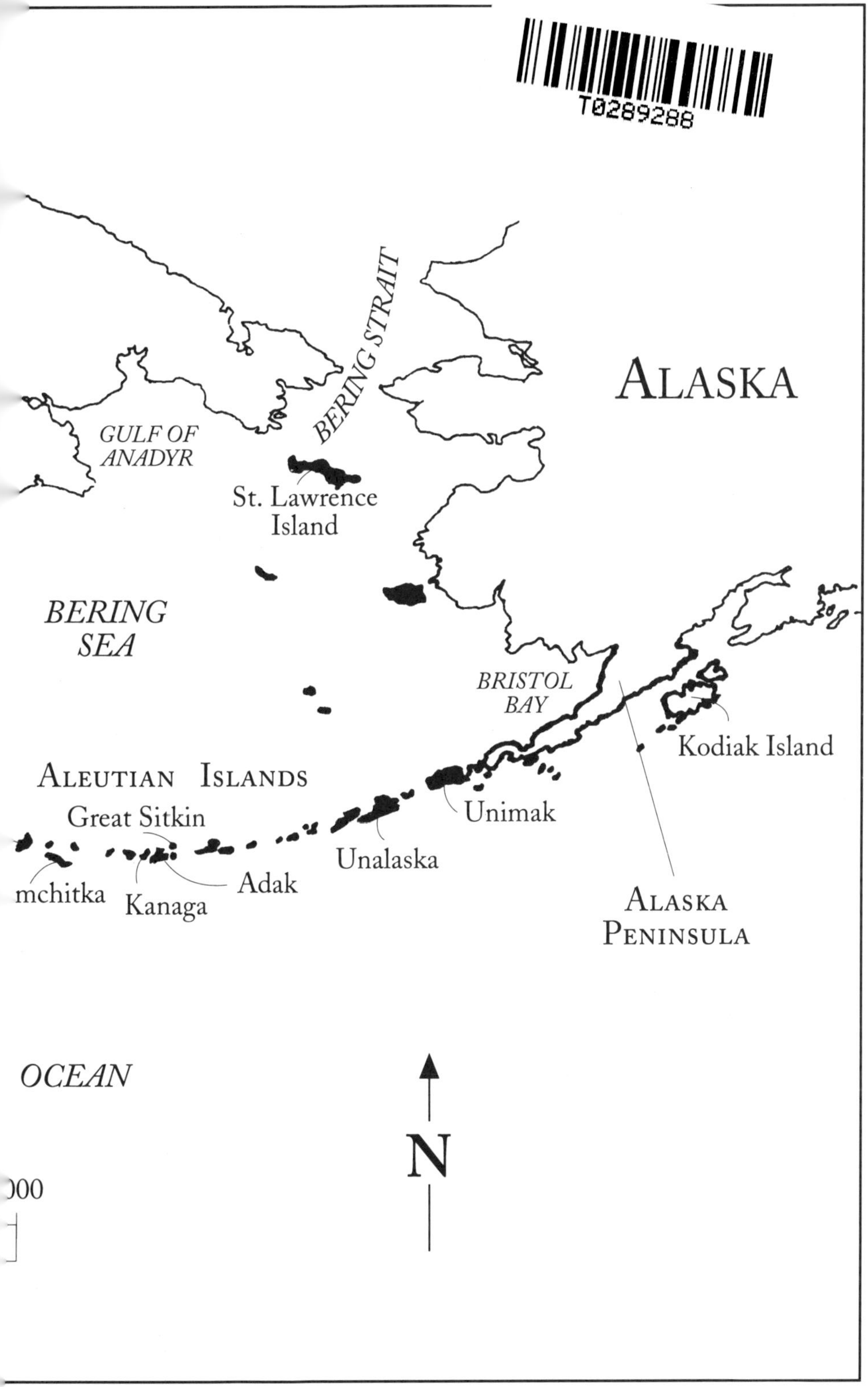
ALASKA
BERING STRAIT
GULF OF ANADYR
St. Lawrence Island
BERING SEA
BRISTOL BAY
Kodiak Island
ALEUTIAN ISLANDS
Great Sitkin
Unimak
Unalaska
Adak
mchitka
Kanaga
ALASKA PENINSULA
OCEAN
N
)00

Aleutian Echoes

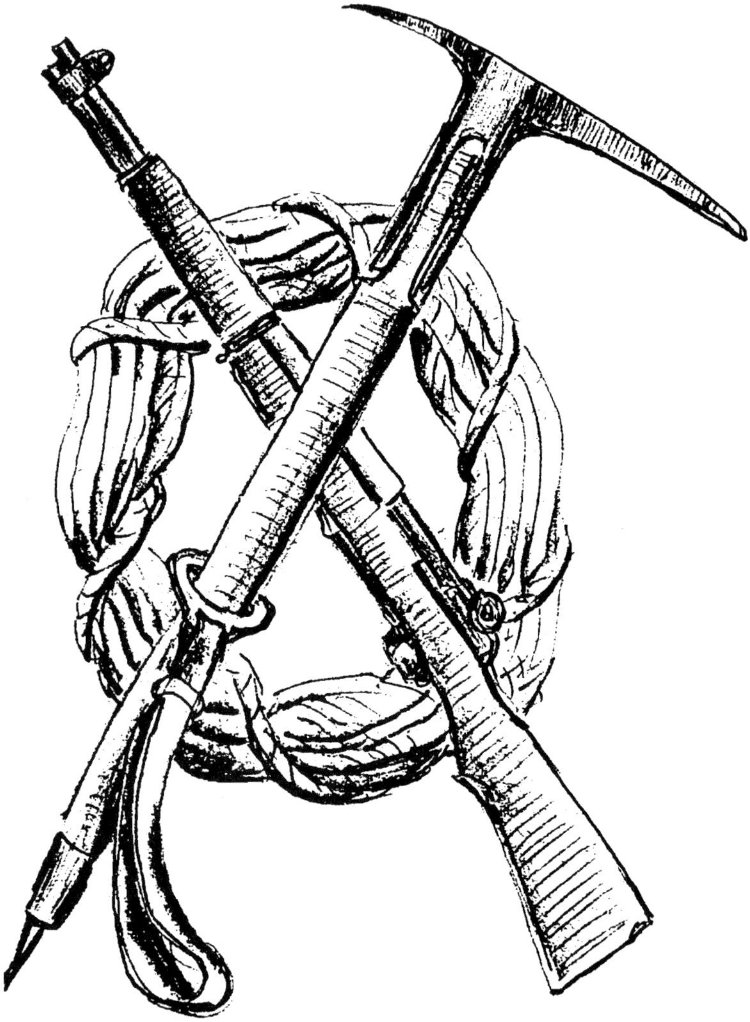

North Pacific Combat School escutcheon displaying crossed ice axe and rifle on a coil of climbing rope.

Aleutian Echoes

Charles C. Bradley

Introduction by Pat Roppel

University of Alaska Press

LanternLight Library

Library of Congress Cataloging-in-Publication Data

Bradley, Charles C., 1911–
Aleutian echoes / Charles C. Bradley ; introduction by Pat Roppel.
p. cm. -- (LanternLight library)
Includes bibliographical references and index.
ISBN 0-912006-74-9: $35.00. -- ISBN 0-912006-75-7 (pbk.) : $25.00
1. Bradley, Charles C., 1911– . 2. World War, 1939– 1945--Campaigns--Alaska--Aleutian Islands. 3. World War, 1939– 1945--Personal narratives, American. 4. Aleutian Islands. 5. United States. Army--Biography. 6. Soldiers--United States--Biography. I. Title. II. Series.
D769.87.A4B73 1994 94-17938
CIP

 First Printing
International Standard Book Number: cloth 0-912006-74-9
paper 0-912006-75-7
Library of Congress Catalogue Number: 94-17938

Printed in Hong Kong by C&C Offset Printing Co., (USA) Inc.

This publication was printed on acid-free paper that meets the minimum requirements for the American National Standard for Information Science—Permanence of Paper for Printed Library Materials ANSI Z39.48-1984

Publication coordination by Pamela Odom.
Cover and book design by Paula Elmes, Publications Center, Center for Cross-Cultural Studies.

All illustrations, unless otherwise noted, are by the author.
The sketch on page 59, "Russian Church on Unalaska," is from the John Muir papers, Holt-Atherton special collections, University of the Pacific Libraries, copyright 1984, Muir-Hanna Trust.

To Pop: who, early on, convinced me that life is a great adventure and that adventure in the mountains is the apex.

And to Nina: my mover-shaker wife who kept this story moving with her arpeggios on the computer key board and by shaking me when needed.

CONTENTS

Part II. Changing Directions

FOREWORD

In this chain of short narratives I have done my best to reconstruct a real World War II adventure with real people in a real time and place. Material for the reconstruction consists of memories, letters home, photographs, and military records. How real are these true stories? Clearly we are looking at varying degrees of approximation. The puzzlement and effort that went into each of these approximations has left me with a strong suspicion that when we probe half-century-old memories for something solid, all we may find are the vestigial emotions of those moments in time—the excitement, the loneliness, the fury, the exhaustion, the laughter, the beauty. These are the truths of memory. Yet these are also what drive me to the writing pad and these are what I really wish to share. The rest is setting, background, and decoration.

C. B.

Acknowledgments

My greatest indebtedness goes to Mike Myers. Back in the days when I was still wondering if there were enough fragments left to build a book around the North Pacific Combat School (NPCS), Mike came bouncing into my life with a bonanza of military archival material on the critical subject of clothing for our troops and the schedule of Jim Ford's flights between Washington, D.C., and Adak to make the clothing happen. Fully as important, Mike put me back in touch with Frank Forrest, commanding officer of NPCS—fifty years ago.

Frank provided many important plugs for my historical gaps, including the origination of NPCS and our original manual of instruction. We compared and consolidated many memories. When we agreed I assumed the truth was in hand—or close enough.

When I was desperately searching for archival information about the NPCS classes, military historian Pierce Mullen suggested I try Tim Menninger in Washington, D.C. Tim instantly put his finger on it. What a relief!

I am indebted to Albert Jackman for a chance to use his final report of the Rainier Expedition as a safety net for the accuracy of my account. And my thanks to Barbara Walton for digging it out of the Resource Center for me.

To Tom and Diana Webb I am indebted for their volume on the war letters of Gordon Stimson who was my buddy when we helped launch the school.

Dee Molenaar generously wedged me into his crowded schedule to produce the artistic maps of Unalaska and Adak. My thanks to Dee.

Thanks also to Margaret Murie for her interesting addition to the puzzle of U.S. military clothing for the battle of Attu.

Finally I should thank Mark Timmerman and the unnamed readers who supported my manuscript and gave helpful advice for its improvement. And the staff of University of Alaska Press that kept things rolling in my favor.

Introduction

In 1940, to meet the increasing Japanese threat in the Pacific, the United States military began a major buildup of forces to provide an adequate defense of the territory of Alaska. Two years later, on June 3, 1942, that threat became a reality when the Japanese attacked Dutch Harbor. Thus, war came to the Aleutian Islands, a little-known part of America.

On the globe, the Aleutian chain appears to provide a natural route of approach toward either the continental United States or Japan. Mountainous, treeless islands extend in a long curve for more than a thousand miles westward from the tip of the Alaska Peninsula.

The islands are of volcanic origin, and several volcanoes are active. The cones have been carved by the gales and heavy seas into jagged peaks that rise abruptly from the seas to elevations of several thousand feet. The lower skirts are covered by a spongy, hummocky mat of grass, forbes, and low shrubs. Above a thousand feet, vegetation yields to naked volcanic rubble, bedrock, snowfields, and glaciers.

In many respects the climate is similar to that of Scotland, which lies at the same latitude, and there is a similar ocean current that ameliorates the temperatures. The late autumn and winter storms are justly famous, with high velocity winds

Aleutian terrain. Official photograph, U.S. Army Air Forces

usually carrying fog and rain mixed with snow. The landscape disappears in a white-out and suddenly the world of mountains is treacherous.

This was the situation that the American and Japanese forces encountered in the Aleutians. The combination of wind, wet, and cold created an insidious and dangerous threat, what is now known as hypothermia. Protective clothing, such as Goretex, was unavailable to the foot soldiers in 1943, as they faced each other on the Aleutian turf.

Pivotal to the military defense of the Aleutian Islands were the navy and army bases at Dutch Harbor, Unalaska. Work on a naval facility began in July 1940. At first, it was thought that Amaknak Island, only 4.3 miles in length, did not possess sufficient level land for the addition of an army base, but a reconsideration resulted in erection of the army base at Margaret Bay, south of Dutch Harbor.[1] The navy's contractor began construction of the army base in January 1941 and barely four months later, on May 8, the first U.S. Army troops arrived. On September 10, 1941, the base was named Fort Mears in honor of Col. Frederick J. Mears, who had been instrumental in surveying and building the Alaska Railroad.

Then on December 7, 1941, the Japanese attacked the United States at Pearl Harbor. The two navy bases at Dutch Harbor and Kodiak Island and the six small posts became vitally important for protection of the Pacific. A great scramble occurred in Alaska as existing bases were upgraded and new bases were constructed.

While the tempo of construction increased as the military prepared to defend Alaska, Japanese military leaders were making plans to further expand its empire; decisions which would impact Alaska's Aleutian Islands.

Adak, looking west across Clam Lagoon and Andrew Lagoon to the base of Mt. Moffet, July 1944. Official photograph, U.S. Army Air Forces

The Japanese planned to seize the two western Aleutian islands so as to secure its northern flank and protect its forces on Midway Island from a possible attack from the north. The object of the Dutch Harbor attack, scheduled one day in advance of the planned air strikes on Midway Island, was to confuse the United States and divert attention.[2]

For its Aleutian operation, the Japanese intended to occupy Adak with army troops, destroy the suspected U.S. garrison there, mine its harbor, and then withdraw its troops to Attu. Kiska was to be occupied with naval forces. Both islands were to be held during the fall, when the occupation forces were to be withdrawn before the onset of winter. The Japanese believed the Aleutians, like its own Kuril Islands, were unfit for bases for sustained operations.

On May 5, 1942, the Imperial Headquarters issued orders for the capture of Midway and the western Aleutians. This set in motion events which culminated in the only campaign fought on American soil during World War II.

Japan's first bombing strike on Alaskan territory took place June 3, 1942, at Dutch Harbor. At this time Bradley was attached to Company A, 87th Mountain Infantry, at Fort Lewis, Washington. Here he listened to the radio announcer tell how, despite a heavy fog and high seas, bombers and fighters were launched from Japanese carriers and how an opening in the clouds provided a window for the pilots to begin bombing and strafing Fort Mears and Dutch Harbor. When the raid was over, the damage to the army and navy bases was minimal. The details of the strike have been covered by a number of military historians.[3]

Despite the unsuccessful raid on Dutch Harbor, the Japanese landed on Reynard Cove on Kiska on the evening of June 6. The next day, troops began to build a garrison and install an elaborate antiaircraft and coastal defense system to protect the newly acquired possession on the North American continent.

The Attu invasion force reached its destination during the morning hours of June 7. Troops pushed overland through the snow and surprised the villagers. After rounding up the Aleuts, the Japanese established their headquarters in the village and began building fortified positions.

Despite the Japanese hope that by bringing the war to the Aleutians it would lure the American Pacific Fleet north, the nearly simultaneous attack on Midway failed. In order to save face and report something successful to the Japanese home front, the Japanese continued to hold onto its Aleutian outposts.[4]

Replanting the Stars and Stripes on Kiska and Attu was the first mission of the Pacific Fleet in 1942. What the Americans needed was a secret base within fighter-plane distance of Kiska. On August 30, 1942, occupation forces landed on Adak, found it unoccupied by Japanese, and located an almost ready-made airfield, a flooded tidal basin. Army engineers drained and filled it in ten days and on September 14, the first Kiska-bound fighter-bomber strike flew off from Adak.

The third major American amphibious assault of World War II was launched against Attu Island on May 11, 1943. After battling 11,000 U.S. troops for nearly three weeks in inclement weather, the remaining Japanese garrison resorted to a banzai charge and those not shot in the attack pulled the pins from grenades attached to their belts. Again, military historians have examined the details of the retaking of Attu.[5]

On Kiska, the Imperial Navy decided to repeat their Guadalcanal evacuation operation. Taking advantage of heavy fog, two cruisers and six destroyers arrived July 28, 1942, and in less than an hour all men were spirited away, taken back to the Kuril Islands undetected. Three weeks after that, when 35,000 American troops stormed ashore onto the barren muskeg, they were astonished to find the enemy gone. Among these men was a detachment of the 10th Mountain Infantry combat troops, but Bradley was not among them.[6]

By the time troops landed on Attu and Kiska, Bradley had finished officer's training and been assigned to the Mountain Training Center at Camp Hale, Colorado. He tells us how unsettling he found it that the Attu forces suffered so terribly from the weather. Little did Bradley realize at the time, that within a year he would be in Alaska training men so this would not happen again. His stay in Alaska was a direct result of this lack of preparation by American troops for inclement climatic conditions.

Many military historians feel the taking of Attu was the high point of the Alaskan war. Kiska was anticlimactic and what happened afterward, as some military historians believe, was chiefly a matter of tying up the loose threads of unfinished business; of deciding upon the role that Alaska and the Aleutians could play in defeating Japan, and of making organizational changes that the situation seemed to require.[7]

This, indeed, was Alaska's military atmosphere when Bradley and the small group detached from the 10th Mountain Infantry came to Dutch Harbor and Fort Mears in June 1944. Here the men would participate in the North Pacific Combat School (NPCS), a mountain warfare school in the Aleutians that would prepare troops in case the United States decided to invade the Kuril Islands.

The Kurils, islands which arch north from Japan's Hokkaido Island toward Siberia's Kamchatka Peninsula, were the site of numerous Japanese military bases, and it was from here that the Pearl Harbor strike force sailed. Most of the bases were located on Paramushiro, the largest of the Kuril Islands, where there were three airfields and the Kashiwabara Army Staging Area.

During the occupation of Attu and Kiska, the Kurils were important. The Japanese realized, after capturing the two American islands, that they must either get out of the Aleutians or strengthen its garrisons, finish the airfields, and attack the enemy supply line. But any such tactics would put an unbearable strain on shipping already depleted by the Guadalcanal campaign and the United States submarines. Yet the Japanese dared not evacuate, thus leaving the Kurils open to American or Russian attack. Imperial Headquarters decided to hold the western Aleutians at all costs and carry out preparations for war in the Kurils.[8] A regular service of freighters had to be maintained in order to build up the garrisons at Attu, 650 miles west, and Kiska, another 378 miles of steaming through stormy waters.

Once the Allies had recovered the western Aleutians, what would they do with them? Should Adak, Kiska, and Attu be used to mount an invasion of Paramushiro? The project was discussed by the Joint Chiefs of Staff (JCS) on September 7, 1943, ten months before Bradley arrived in Alaska. A negative recommendation was made.[9] The capture of Paramushiro would require more forces than could be spared, with the Gilberts and Bougainville invasions timed for November. Possession of the Kurils would be of no benefit to the Allies unless it was exploited for a further advance into Hokkaido Island, a project which had been rejected. Paramushiro in enemy hands was only a minor threat to the Aleutians.

However, a month later on October 5, 1943, the JCS approved a gradual strengthening of the western Aleutians, with a view of a possible Paramushiro operation depending upon whether the Russians entered the war against Japan, upon the status and progress of other Pacific operations, and upon the availability of shipping.[10] The War Department accordingly directed that a plan be made for an assault on Paramushiro with the target date, for planning purposes, set for the spring of 1945.[11]

Since the weather and terrain of the Kuril Islands was believed to be similar to that of the Aleutians, the military did not want a repeat of the climatic agony suffered by its troops during

Looking north by west, Hidden Bay in the foreground, Mt. Moffet in the background. Official photograph, U.S. Army Air Forces

the battle of Attu, thus, it authorized the North Pacific Combat School. It was only fitting that the experience of the 10th Mountain Infantry Division, to which Bradley was attached, be included in this school.

The 10th Mountain Infantry Division originated when several outdoor groups, especially the National Ski Association, showed concern about American military forces who were trained and geared for flatlands and the jungle. If the U.S. had to face Hitler's Alpine troops in Europe, would U.S. troops know how to outmaneuver them? Skiers wrote President Franklin D. Roosevelt and Secretary of War Henry L. Stinson in vain. Then in 1940, Charles Minot Dole of the National Ski Patrol convinced the military that Americans on skis could defend the Rockies just as the Finns had defended their country.[12] Through Dole's perseverance, this civilian ski association was hired by the War Department to help recruit men with special talents for military duty.[13] As a result, Company A, 87th Infantry Mountain Regiment, was activated at Fort Lewis, Washington, November 15, 1941, and the men, including Bradley, trained at 14,408-foot Mt. Rainier.

In the six months from March to September 1942, the Army Ground Forces launched four special installations, one of which was the Mountain Training Center.[14] When it was decided to expand the 87th Mountain Infantry Regiment, the National Ski Association, in May 1942, sent a notice to all members and others with specialized talents to aid in recruiting "men accustomed to living and working in the high mountains—packers, prospectors, trappers, Forest Service men, timber cruisers, guides, and men who have made mountaineering an avocation—whether or not they can ski."[15]

Camp Hale, a subpost of Camp Carson, Colorado, was created in the Rocky Mountains 150 miles west of Colorado Springs for the Mountain Training Center. The center's mission was to test equipment, formulate requirements within the field of its specialty, and supervise the special training of standard military units.[16]

At the Mountain Training Center, a few specially designated mountain units were assembled. The 10th Light Division (Pack, Alpine), centering around the 87th Mountain Infantry Regiment, was activated July 15, 1943.[17]

After barely a year of testing and training, the Army Ground Forces, believing the division had produced negative results and fearing administrative complications in maintaining a single special-type mountain division, recommended in May 1944 that the 10th Light Division be reorganized as a standard infantry division. The War Department agreed.[18] Bradley describes the decision he and members of the North Pacific Combat School were required to make because of this reorganization.

The men of the 10th Light Division embarked for Italy in December 1944 after being redesignated as the 10th Mountain Division in November. It fought in campaigns in the North Apennines and Po Valley.

By the time the former 10th Light Division embarked for Italy, the North Pacific Combat School was located at the Adak military base. The school had been at Fort Mears from June until August 1944. This change from Fort Mears to Adak came because, by the summer of 1944, the war had moved far from Unalaska. Although Dutch Harbor continued to monitor Soviet ships and dispatch air and sea patrols in the North Pacific, Fort Mears had fulfilled its original missions. No longer was there a threat of any enemy attack. In August, the post was placed on a housekeeping status.

Adak was an enormous facility when the North Pacific Combat School arrived there. After the Japanese were cleared from the Aleutians, the Alaska Defense Command made preparations to build a supply base on Adak capable of equipping and maintaining an expeditionary force of 50,000 men. Although work began in October 1943, it was still continuing in 1944.[19]

Throughout the existence of the North Pacific Combat School, the officers continued their mission to prepare men for the invasion of the Kuril Islands.

Other military forces in Alaska were involved with the Kurils. During 1944 and 1945, the North Pacific Force harassed the Japanese defenses of the Kuril Islands. Medium and heavy bombers flew about 1,500 sorties against the Kurils before the end of the war.[20]

As the North Pacific Combat School trained instructors in "amphibious, mountain and muskeg combat techniques," Joseph Stalin and Franklin D. Roosevelt at Yalta agreed upon the terms for Soviet intervention in the war. The Soviet Union finally declared war on Japan on August 8, 1945. The Eleventh Air Force flew its last bombing mission from Shemya on the Aleutians to Paramushiro on August 13. Two days later Japan surrendered.

The plan for an invasion of the Kuril Islands, possibly using troops who had learned to successfully cope with the northern weather and terrain, was not implemented. With the immediate confusion of the end of World War II, the North Pacific Combat School continued to train instructors. Its last group were all black and according to Bradley, came from troops already stationed in Alaska. Probably all or many of these were from the 364th Infantry Regiment, an all-black group which was rotated to the Aleutians in March 1944 in place of the 140th Infantry Regiment. It performed garrison duties for the rest of the war.[21] The inclusion of blacks in the North Pacific Combat School illustrates a change of attitude from 1942 when the Quartermaster General urged that no Negro troops, indeed no troops who had not been inured to life in cold climates, be sent to the Far North.[22]

Bradley experiences some of the chaos which took place in Alaska on many of the bases at the conclusion of the war. By that time, Alaska's military activity had slowed. Dutch Harbor's submarine facility had been decommissioned in May 1945; the air station had been reduced to a naval air facility in June of that year. Fort Mears had been on housekeeping status for over a year.

Even before Bradley was released from the army in 1946, the 10th Light Division and Company A, 87th Infantry (an element of the 10th Light Division) had been inactivated in November 1945 at Camp Carson, Colorado.[23]

Today, the military still has a presence in Alaska but not on Amaknak Island. Today the Ounalashka Native Corporation, formed by the Aleuts after the Alaska Native Land Claims Settlement Act, holds title to nearly all the land where the former military bases at Dutch Harbor and Fort Mears stood. Unalaska was a tiny Native village at the time the military arrived prior to World War II. Now the city of Unalaska includes all of Amaknak Island as well as the original community and is the most populated of all the communities in southwest Alaska.

The city of Unalaska is the proprietor of the navy's giant wartime power plant, the navy's airstrip is paved, and the state of Alaska operates the airport for both commercial and charter air companies. The submarine base has been converted into an industrial area for the fishing industry. The army's pier at Chernofski is used for storage of commercial crab pots. Some of the officers' quarters have been converted into residences. Many other military structures have disappeared or deteriorated beyond recovery.

Adak is still in service today and is one of the world's most costly and remote military operations.[24] In 1948 it changed from control by the army to the air force. In 1950, the navy took over custody from the air force. In 1951, a Naval Communications Station was established and in November 1977, the Naval Facility Adak was commissioned. In April 1977, when the Naval Security Group Adak was commissioned, it took over all communications functions. Today one-half of the island is military land and the other half is part of the Aleutian Islands Unit, Alaska Maritime National Wildlife Refuge.

—PAT ROPPEL
SITKA, ALASKA

NOTES

1. Sandra McDermott Faulkner and Robert L. S. Spude, *Naval Operating Base, Dutch Harbor and Fort Mears, Unalaska Island, Alaska* (Anchorage: National Park Service, Alaska Region, 1987): 12–13.

2. John Haile Cloe, *The Air Force in Alaska, Part II: Build-up to Dutch Harbor, June 1940–June 1942* (Elmendorf Air Force Base, Alaska: Office of History Alaskan Air Command, 1986): 148–49.

3. Brian Garfield, *The Thousand-Mile War: World War II in Alaska and the Aleutians* (New York: Ballantine Books, 1973); John Haile Cloe, *The Aleutian Warriors: A History of the 11th Air Force & Fleet Air Wing 4, Part I* (Anchorage, Alaska/Missoula, Montana: Anchorage Chapter—Air Force Association and Pictorial Histories Publishing Company, Inc., 1991).

4. David Bergamini, *Japan's Imperial Conspiracy* (New York: William Morrow and Company, Inc., 1971): 984.

5. John Costello, *The Pacific War* (New York: Rawson, Wade Publishers, Inc., 1981); David Bergamini, *Japan's Imperial Conspiracy*; Dashiell Hammett and Robert Colodny, *The Battle of the Aleutians 1942–43 in the Capture of Attu: Tales of World War II in Alaska As Told By the Men Who Fought There* (Anchorage: Alaska Northwest Publishing Company, 1984).

6. Curtis W. Casewit, *Mountain Troopers! The Story of the 10th Mountain Division* (New York: Thomas Y. Crowell Company, 1972): 10–16.

7. Stetson Conn, Rose C. Engelman, and Byron Fairchild, *Guarding the United States and Its Outposts* (Washington, D.C.: Office of the Chief of Military History, 1964): 298.

8. Samuel Eliot Morison, *Aleutians, Gilberts and Marshalls: June 1942–April 1944* (Boston: Little, Brown and Company, 1990): 18; Bergamini, *Japan's Imperial Conspiracy*, 986.

9. Ibid., p. 65.

10. Maurice Matloff, *Strategic Planning for Coalition Warfare 1943–1944* (Washington, D.C.: Office of the Chief of Military History, 1959): 316–17.

11. Conn et al., pp. 298–99.

12. Winston Pote, *Mountain Troops: 10th Mountain Division, Camp Hale, Colorado* (Camden, Maine: Down East Books, 1982): 2–4.

13. John K. Mahon and Romana Danysh, *Infantry: Part I: Regular Army*, Army Lineage Series (Washington, D.C.: Office of the Chief of Military History, 1972): 767.

14. Kent Roberts Greenfield, Robert R. Palmer, and Bell I. Wiley, *The Organization of Group Combat Troops, US Army in World War II* (Washington, D.C.: Historical Division, Department of the Army, 1947): 340.

15. Pote, p. 1.

16. Greenfield et al., p. 340.

17. John B. Wilson, *Armies, Corps, Divisions, and Separate Brigades*, Army Lineage Series (Washington, D.C.: Center of Military History, 1987): 257.

18. Greenfield et al., pp. 348–349.

19. Karl C. Dod, *The Corps of Engineers: The War against Japan* (Washington, D.C.: Office of the Chief of Military History, 1966): 334.

20. Garfield, p. 342–343.

21. Ulysses Lee, *The Employment of Negro Troops, US Army in WW II* (Washington, D.C.: Office of the Chief of Military History, 1966): 370, 472.

22. Ibid., p. 440.

23. Wilson, p. 257.

24. Stan Cohen, *The Forgotten War, A Pictorial History of World War II in Alaska and Northwestern Canada,* Vol. 3 (Missoula, Montana: Pictorial Histories Publishing Company, 1992): 200.

Part I

Early Directions

Preceding page: Mt. Moffet ski ascent, Adak

An Autobiography

I grew up in Madison, Wisconsin, the first of seven boys. Father (Pop) was head of the Department of Physiological Chemistry at the University of Wisconsin. In summer his research activities took him (and his family) to Woods Hole, Massachusetts, and the Marine Biological Laboratory. It was there we got a taste of the sea—sea fishing, sea faring, and seafood. But Pop was also a mountain man, having grown up in Berkeley, California, in the shadow of the Sierra Nevada where one of the high peaks carries his father's name. Pop could not bear to be gone from his mountains for more than two or three years at a time. On his Sierra summers he took with him any of his sons who could walk. Mother (Mom) was usually there, too. Mom, granddaughter of the founder of the Crane Company, grew up in Chicago. She was completely deaf but had learned to read lips and was more independent than most women of the time. When she married Pop, he took her straight out of Chicago's Loop into the wild north country of Lake Timagami. A few weeks later, she returned a confirmed outdoor woman, able to sleep on the ground and skillful with a canoe paddle. In due time she also became a mountain woman.

In Wisconsin, surrounded as we were with wild Nordic ski jumpers, we learned the arts of ski jumping, cross-country racing and ski touring, and we began to dream of ski touring in the Sierras. My chance came in February 1935 when I graduated from the University of Wisconsin with a bachelor's degree in geology. To celebrate, Pop and I took a six-day ski camping trip across the Sierras from Mono Lake to Yosemite Valley. I was hooked. From then on I tried to think of ways to make a living without ever leaving the snowy mountains. When World War II came along with the creation of the 10th Mountain Infantry Division, I wormed my way in. For five years I had my wish, although the nature of my employment was not exactly what I had in mind.

Trail to Mystery

In July of 1941 war with Germany seemed imminent. I closed down my photographic business in Madison, Wisconsin, and enlisted in the army. With me were my brother Steve and a ski-jumping buddy, Billy Neidner. We had consecutive serial numbers. Very shortly, Steve, a motion picture photographer, was on his way to the Signal Corps training film headquarters in Ft. Monmouth, New Jersey. Then Billy was assigned to Camp Walter, Texas.

As for me, with my training in both geology and photography, and since I also carried a private pilot's license, I applied for the Army Mapping Service. The Selective Service was enthusiastic about this prospect—until they discovered I was over twenty-eight years of age and thus, under mapping service regulations, ineligible. So they assigned me to the Medical Service at Camp Grant, Illinois, where neither my advanced

Billy Neidner at Camp Grant, Illinois

age nor my lack of medical background seemed to be of much concern.

This solution by the Selective Service was my first military jolt. More would follow. For instance, my first assignment was as part of a four-man crew building boardwalks around Camp Grant. The work was not difficult except for the required velocity. We had to stay ahead of another crew that was just behind us and had the advantage of heavy equipment. Their assignment was to tear up the boardwalk in order to lay storm sewer pipes.

Privates Charles and Steve Bradley, just inducted. Camp Grant, Illinois

My gamesmanship developed rapidly. In a short time I took my first step toward becoming a four-star general. Corporal Bradley, they now called me.

In spite of my new rank and power, there was a gnawing thought below the surface that I had somehow managed to walk into a quagmire that was getting quaggier every day. You can imagine my burst of hope when I read a military news release reporting an army decision to create an infantry unit trained for mountain and winter warfare. Certain citizens were assisting the army in rounding up candidates already familiar with snowy mountains. These would become the nucleus for training. The most miraculous item of the news release was the name of a citizen assistant who was a friend of mine. That night a letter was written and posted in secrecy. We soldiers were supposed to make such requests through channels only.

About this time Japan bombed Pearl Harbor and World War II was on. Clamor and confusion prevailed, and this may well have helped my cause. A couple of weeks later, while the uproar still dominated, my commanding officer (C.O.) called me in. He looked pretty tense.

"Corporal Bradley, I have orders to transfer you immediately to the Ski Troops at Ft. Lewis, Washington. Do you know anything about this?"

Corporal Bradley: "Well—um—no, sir—um—I've never heard of the Ski Troops." That *was* the truth—sorta.

C.O., with evident irritation: "Well, that's my orders and that's where you are going. Pack your bags, *Private* Bradley. You will be leaving by train tomorrow. That is all."

Corporal Bradley—now busted to private for his sins—left the building light of heart and foot. He spoke thus to himself: "Ski troops, wow! Oh please, please, sir, don't throw me into that briar patch."

Uneasiness set in very soon after I had stepped off the bus at Ft. Lewis. It was some time before I found anyone who went beyond "Ski Troops? Mountain Troops? Never heard of 'em—sorry." That was in part because their headquarters in "Old" Ft. Lewis was some distance from "New" Ft. Lewis where I landed. It was also in part because the name of the unit was "The 87th Infantry Regiment re-enforced." When I finally found them, there were only a handful of candidates who had arrived. I doubt if any of us at that time sensed that we were in the first dozen or so that would become a force of more than 10,000 in two years.

Several old friends were on hand to welcome me aboard. Of all people, Pvt. Billy Neidner, who had disappeared from Camp

Beginning class, downhill skiing, Paradise

Captain Paul Lafferty, Company A, 87th Mountain Infantry

Grant, Illinois, en route to Camp Walter, Texas, now reappeared as Corporal Neidner, a squad leader in Company B, 87th Infantry Re-enforced. Private Bradley attained promotions in due time but he never did catch up to Billy Neidner.

Men assigned to the 87th were arriving daily. Company A, my outfit, was under the command of Capt. Paul Lafferty. What luck! Paul was one of the best mountain men and best leaders I ever met. His instruction was largely by example, but when words were needed he used them frugally and quietly, usually with a smile and an intense look that suggested the words best not be forgotten.

It was midwinter, which in Ft. Lewis by-the-sea means rain and fog, while on Mt. Rainier a few miles to the east it means heavy snowfalls. The 87th was rolled up and transported by bus to Paradise, a recreation area on the south slope of Mt. Rainier where the well-plowed roads lay in snow canyons deeper than the buses and where my quarters on the first floor of the lodge required me to climb to the third floor to step out of doors. Paradise? Right on! A place to study war? Too weird to think about.

In a fairly short time the men were sorted out as trainers or trainees and the training began. Some of the best in the nation were among the trainers. Some of the skiers had been Olympic contestants. Most of these instructors came from the mountainous parts of the nation, California, Oregon, Washington in the west, New Hampshire, Vermont, Maine in the east. There was a fair amount of noisy competitiveness among these groups. Those of us from the Midwest had been ski jumpers (of no military value) and cross-country racers. A few of us had the suspicion that skiing in any military operation was going to be ninety-nine percent slogging uphill with heavy packs, but we spoke very quietly and learned downhill techniques as fast as possible. It was rare sport. Though I never became a downhill expert, I was able to help beginners through the early stages—and I became a corporal again.

Once in a while Captain Lafferty would take the whole company on a long tour through the ups and downs, the glades and woods around Paradise. In part these tours were to develop lungs and legs, and in part to indicate that a mountain soldier has many things to learn beside barreling down hill. On these tours we carried packs, lightly loaded with extra clothing, matches, food, light sleeping bags, and other necessities. As time went on the loads increased to include overnight and cooking equipment. Our backs and shoulders were toughening up and we were learning some of the difficulties arising from barreling down hill with a heavy load riding high on our backs that has its own inertia, power, and direction. When we were finally carrying rifles, a common misjudgment of speed and control could end in the load lifting the skier off the snow, rolling him forward in the air, and driving him head first back into the snow. The rifle, lagging slightly, would now catch up and deliver the *coup de grace* by whacking the skier on the head and driving him still deeper into the snow.

One evening, after one of Captain Lafferty's long tours with heavy packs, Company A was ready to mutiny. From their quarters came a barrage of loud complaints about aching backs, chafed shoulders, bumps on the head, exhaustion, frosted fingers, inhuman leadership, to name a few. It was loud enough to be heard easily by the captain as he strolled in, set his pack down, and shed his outdoor clothing. He looked very much as he did when we left in the early dawn light.

He greeted me with his usual smile and asked how things were going with my squad. I told him we had had a good workout and I, for one, was ready to sit down. He nodded. We chatted some more. Then he said, "Oh, by the way, I've been trying out a new rucksack. It seems to work pretty well. Why don't you try it on and see how it feels." So I walked over and reached down for the pack. At first I thought it had been nailed to the floor. It was all I could do to get it on to my back. "What do you think?" he asked casually. After some wrestling I finally got it off my back and on to the floor. "Wow!" I said, "What do you have in there?" His eyebrows went up a little, "Oh, that," he smiled slightly. "I always put in a few rocks so as to keep fit for combat loads."

Of course he knew I'd pass that news back to the rest of the company. Without his saying a word to the company, the bitching faded away on the night wind.

I can recall one other time when the leading edge of mutiny was visible in the 87th. That was the day our commanding officer, Col. Onslow S. Rolfe, ordered the entire regiment to lay down its skis and strap on snowshoes.

Just why the colonel issued such an order I never knew, but here are a couple of guesses. First, he thought there was more recreation taking place on the mountainside than preparation for combat, and it was time to shake things up. Second, he was concerned about the amount of time it takes to make skiers out of nonskiers. Snowshoers could do most of the required job with much less training and with no poles to carry. (These thoughts are actually my own as you will see later in the story—two years later, in fact. On a different scale and under different circumstances, I was facing the ski-snowshoe dilemma.)

The day Sven was born

Forget the reasons. Be it known that when Colonel Rolfe gave his famous order, at least 150 jaws dropped in unison and the word *WHAT!* rolled across the land and echoed off the glaciers of Rainier. Was military skiing to die aborning? Was the colonel so insensitive as not to feel the disdain a good skier holds for snowshoeing? Was he trying to insult his regiment?

Well, no matter. That *was* the day the 87th walked around Paradise on snowshoes. That was also the day some of the men discovered that on a steep snowy hillside, snowshoes were a disaster. They made sure that when the colonel came by with his notebook, they were on a steep snowy hillside where men floundered around and fell sideways, unable to free themselves from their buried snowshoes. What a shambles!

That evening our singing group gathered in earnest. Before midnight there emerged the ballad of "Sven" in four-part harmony for male voices. Before morning, most of the regiment knew the words and could sing along and, at breakfast, did so mightily.

Because there may be no better example of the power of music, and because this song was a favorite in the mountain troops, and because I later heard many people of either sex singing it with no real idea of where it came from, I here reproduce the ballad in its entirety for the sake of history.

Sven

(To the music of "A Bold Bad Man")

Oola had a cousin from the wild and wooly west.
While Oola liked the skiing, Sven liked snowshoeing the best.
They got into the Mountain Troops to put it to a test
And every where they went they gave their war whoop.

Chorus

Oh give me skis and some poles and klister
*And let me ski way up on Alta Vista.**
You can take your snowshoes and burn them, sister
And everywhere I go you'll hear my war whoop.

Everyone was keen to see how it would all come out,
The Winter Warfare Board was standing anxiously about,
And even Axis agents had been sent up there to scout
And everyone was waiting for the war whoop.

Chorus

The Colonel pulled the trigger and they started out to race.
Sven got an early start and set a most terrific pace
But Oola skied right by him with a sneer upon his face
And when he reached the top he gave his war whoop.

---

*Alta Vista—a high promontory about Paradise.

Chorus

Two seconds later Oola finished in a mighty schuss
Passing on the way poor Sven a-lying on his puss.
The moral of this story is that snowshoes have no use
And poor old Sven no longer gives his war whoop.

Chorus

(Addendum)
The 87th had a Heavy Weapons Company.
They spent six weeks at Paradise but never learned to ski.
The reason for this tragedy, as you can plainly see
Is every where they went they wore their snowshoes.

Chorus

The colonel was actually rather proud of his 87th choral group. When he heard the song he had a good laugh. Sven disappeared from the 87th, except for the heavy weapons company; few skiers could make good use of their skis while carrying such heavy loads. Snowshoes give more predictable footing, although they have their own limitations.

It was during the early training period that I became aware of the Mountain and Winter Warfare Board. Its purpose was to be sure that these future mountain soldiers had appropriate training, clothing, equipment and food for their special assignment. It seemed a daunting problem to start from scratch and build a solid support system for a brand-new fighting arm. It meant new supply bridges between industry and army, new technique bridges between civilian experts and military tacticians; finally there was the need for bridges between old army and new army.

The president of the board was our regimental commander Colonel Rolfe, but the actual coordination of this brain-breaking assignment was Capt. Albert Jackman, a lean artillery man temporarily derailed from the big guns because of his hobby of

Captain Albert Jackman

climbing mountains. A soldier and mountaineer: a good first bridge.

One of the first things I noticed about Captain Jackman was his eternal habit of pulling out a small notebook and writing something into it. Strange that it always appeared to be the same notebook but it never got fatter. What was in there? It could have been that question or something like it that lured me into Captain Jackman's operation and I got caught in the machinery—helping with tests and evaluations of food and equipment. I always did have a weakness for food.

The climax of this association came when I was included in a twelve-day expedition into the upper reaches of Mt. Rainier, leading finally to the summit of this king of mountains. The main objectives of the expedition were to test food and equipment under conditions far more severe than those at Paradise. Coincidentally we would be learning the arts of survival and mobility, under these same conditions, which included rough mountain terrain, glaciers, fierce winds, heavy snowstorms, and the threat of avalanches.

Each of us had an assignment of duties. For instance, Captain Jackman was C.O. and Lt. Paul Townsend was second in command. Lt. John Jay kept weather records and was photographer. S.Sgt. Ralph Wiese was our medic and kept records of food consumption. I helped in food consumption records and was in charge of daily radio communications with Paradise base. Cpl. Peter Gabriel was in charge of mountaineering instruction and was assisted by Cpl. Eldon Metzger. Pvt. Paul Estes assisted where needed. Various detachments from the 87th supported the expedition, acting as porters who helped boost the sixty-pound loads of material to be tested as far as Camp Muir, several thousand feet above Paradise. From there on, the loads would be boosted, tested and evaluated by the expedition members. The merry month of May sounds like spring and to some extent spring could be detected in the air at Paradise, but our binoculars told us that up on the mountain, winter was still in command. On May 8, as we started up the slope with climbers on our skis, I caught a glimpse of the summit through a hole in the clouds. I had never been in such a place. It seemed almost straight overhead, a detached mass of ice, rock and swirling snow, floating in the sky, inaccessible, threatening, beckoning.

En route to Camp Muir

We arrived at Camp Muir in the early afternoon, porters and all. We put all the loads in the sturdy little guide's cabin, the last building we would see until the expedition ended. The porters then took off in swirling snow plumes for Paradise. It was quiet; we were bone tired and ready to drop. Up slope a little way from the cabin we pitched our tents, cooked a hasty supper and crawled into our bags, too exhausted to sleep. This was Camp 1. We had taken our first step toward the summit.

For the next two days a heavy snowstorm gave us a chance to rest, catch up, and get organized again. Without knowing

Corporal Eldon Metzger (ski climbers)

Private Paul Estes (crampons)

Lieutenant John Jay

Sergeant Ralph Wiese

Captain Albert Jackman and Lieutenant Paul Townsend

it immediately, we had already run three important tests on equipment.

The first test started with a few of the gang who developed severe headaches during the first twenty-four hours. A radio conference with the doctor at Paradise led to the thought that carbon monoxide from a couple of new untested gasoline cookstoves might explain it. We immediately stopped use of those stoves and the headaches disappeared. So we sent a request for two replacements from another brand of stove. A couple of days later two members of the support team brought the bundle of new stoves up. They worked okay. End of test.

Corporal Charles Bradley

The next two tests were really two in one—a comparison of two styles of tent for ski troopers on the move. The first was a simple four-sided pyramid, with a central support pole and perimeter pegs to hold down the skirts. It accommodated two men and their gear very comfortably. It was tall enough in the central area for both men to stand erect, and there was a waterproof floor to protect sleeping bags.

The other test involved identical twin tents that could be used together or separately. Each sheltered two men. When pitched they looked like a couple of cloth doghouses for very long-legged dogs. In fact the World War I pup tent came to mind as a probable distant ancestor. As if to avoid any such bad press, these tents were named Everest tents or Meade tents and if truly they *were* related to the pup tents, evolution had been very busy in those twenty-five years. For that style of tent the steep sloping roof was unusually high—high enough so one man could stand if he didn't mind stooping. When two of these tents were used together, face to face zipper flaps became a tunnel connection that could be used as joint cooking space and extra storage. These tents, too, had waterproof floors. Feeling wonderfully snug, we in the Everest tents listened to the whisper of a snowstorm getting underway.

By morning a couple of feet of snow had been added to the landscape. We four in the Everest tents had a leisurely breakfast and then donned our winter clothes, opened the flap, and pushed our way out into an alpine fairy land. Looking over at the pyramid tent, we could see that we had a productive first test. Underneath the cap of snow the tent had the appearance of a slender steeple with the top bent over. From the tent came noises of men at work, which was verified by heaving bulges and shakings within the steeple. Also from within came vocal observations and evaluations of the tent, delivered with force and candor.

It seems that the new snow, sliding off the roof during the night, gathered on the edge of the skirt and gradually piled up there, flattening the skirt and encroaching on the inner space. In addition, of course, the apex of the tent was increasingly under a vertical down pull, until the center pole bent over. Then, of course, the falling snow really went to work. The load encroached on the sleeping bags and the men within. The men awoke, got the drift, so to speak, and gathered around the base of the pole. By morning they found it very hard to move. We helped evacuate the prisoners.

Clearly this pyramid tent was unsatisfactory, as it stood, for snow and winter camping. In the Everest tents we had very little problem with snow encroachment. There were at least two reasons for that. With much less perimeter and floor space there was less of a snow load. Also the tents had a favorable design factor. The bottom one foot of the skirt was a low wall with an *overhang* maintained by cords and stakes. That, combined with the tall steep roof, kept most of the accumulating snow out away from the bottom of the tent. The pyramid tent redesigned with a two-foot overhanging wall might well be improved. A large tent would be more useful in a base camp than on the march. To me the Everest tent looked hard to beat, and I recall urging it strongly for the 10th Mountain Division.

Thus our test work began. The fact that we never saw the Everest again doesn't mean we lost it all. In due time the army unveiled what it called "Tent, Mountain," somewhat similar to "Tent, Everest." Being still civilians at heart, we nicknamed it mountain tent. Instead of a zipper flap it had a fabric tunnel. After the inhabitants entered the tent through the tunnel, it could be gathered and tied like a sack. This was an improvement over Everest in that zippers are prone to various kinds of failures which create problems, sometimes serious ones. Unfortunately the tunnel did not lend itself to combining two tents, but that was not serious. When the tunnel was gathered and tied, its appearance strongly suggested what it was later named, "The Navel."

The mountain tent was more squat than Everest and had no overhanging wall at the base. Later these factors proved to be serious omissions, but by that time I was no longer with the 10th Mountain Infantry. I was in a corner of the world far from the 10th, an area where many items, especially items of clothing and shelter, were out of tune and sometimes performed badly.

On May 11, we started the search for a suitable site for Camp 2 as high as possible above Camp 1, keeping it within a half day's climb. All we found this day was a route to no such place. We

Camp 1, pyramid tents

En route to Camp 2

were back at Camp 1 in time for shelter from a snowstorm riding a screeching wind. The next day the storm was still in progress and wind slab was developing. A layer of wind-consolidated snow over loose snow may be subject to fracture and avalanche. Mountain lore suggested that we sit tight for another day. We did and that gave us time to dry out our wet gear in the bright sunlight without feeling guilty.

On May 14, we divided up into two groups and roped up, four on a rope. One was led by Peter Gabriel, the other by Eldon Metzger. Each rope took a different route up the steepening slope with a prescribed rendezvous higher up. We would be on glaciers, and glaciers have crevasses. After heavy snowstorms the crevasse may be bridged by snow, creating a wicked trap for a lone man on foot or skis. On a rope the man is protected and could be rescued by his buddies. After we had rendezvoused we found our site for Camp 2. It looked crazy to me, but with a little coaxing I bought the logic. This was the reasoning: Probably our greatest threat was avalanches, and they certainly were fearsome. From Paradise I had seen a huge avalanche run for a couple of miles down the lower slopes of Rainier. The sustained roar and exploding clouds of snow were impressive signals of energy on the loose. Avalanches tend to run in chutes, carved out of the rock by glacial tongues or melt water from glaciers, or by the avalanches themselves. To avoid avalanches up here meant finding a site on the knife-edge ridges between the chutes.

Our two mountain instructors finally found a snowy niche just below the crest of a black volcanic blade. We carved out a flat shelf in the snow, which was almost ice, and used the blocks to give us a protective rim on the outer edge. It was a spectacular observation porch as well as a solid place for tents and somewhat protected from wind. I found myself praying that the basal

Cover of American Ski Annual *showing Camp 2 on "Rolfe Cleaver," Mt. Rainier*

snow would not shear off, taking us, tents and all, on a long vertical flight down to the glacier a hundred or so feet below. My prayers were answered and we enjoyed our eagle nest. So we named it "Rolfe Cleaver" for Colonel Rolfe. We were now 12,300 feet above sea level.

The party returned to Camp 1 for the night.

The next morning, in spite of unfavorable weather, we decided to move camp to the new site. After all, the trail was well marked with orange colored wands. By suppertime the transfer was completed and tents were up. The night was windless and clear but the temperature dropped to 3°F. In spite of the heavy day's work, no one slept very well.

May 16 was a good day to go to the summit. The weather was favorable. The minimum loads would make this a day of rest and relaxation. Peter Gabriel, our senior mountaineer, took the lead on Rope 1. Captain Jackman was second man on that rope, and I was third. Rope 2 was led by Eldon Metzger. They planted orange wands to mark the trail in case the weather shut down. The wands were inserted at rope-length intervals.

We had not gone very far before Peter, probing with his ice axe, discovered he was on the edge of a crevasse with a roof of snow. Captain Jackman jammed his ice axe down into the snow pack, took several turns of rope around the handle, and stood by to belay Peter if he fell through. Peter proceeded to cut a few steps down the face of the crevasse to where he could step across the crack; then he cut steps up the other side. When he was across, the rest of us, belayed by Peter, crossed on his steps. It was a nice impromptu demonstration.

Soon we were on glacial ice. We attached crampons to our boots and proceeded up the ice dome toward the summit, leaving a long row of orange wands as the only visible landmarks.

Corporal Peter Gabriel cuts steps across hidden crevasse

Finally at the summit, elevation 14,000+ feet and way above the cloud deck, we stood on the crown of the king. From there we could see the rest of the army of volcanic cones, strung out to the south, visible almost across the face of Oregon. Their white summits were well above the crest of the Cascade Range on which they all stood, a mountain range on top of a mountain range. We were looking at a small sector of what is known as the Ring of Fire, a belt of volcanoes that encircles the Pacific Ocean. At that moment I could not know that in two years I would be living on another sector of the Ring of Fire.

Peter Gabriel completes crossing

On our descent, we learned for life the wisdom of planting the orange wands. A thick fog suddenly settled down on us. Visibility was less than a rope's length. When a wand was sighted, the last man on the rope anchored himself there, while the leader went out the length of the rope and searched for the next wand. In one scary period the leader could not locate a wand. It had probably blown away. What to do? The leader attached Rope 2 and went out two lengths in hopes of finding the next wand. It took quite a while but he finally did find it, and the rest of the descent to Camp 2 was without incident.

May 17. It may sound like an unbelievable inversion, but this was the day we started our descent to Paradise.

Clouds and snowfall would have made the move very difficult and hazardous had not the trail been well marked with

Rainier summit. Rope 2 gang below

orange wands. It was hazardous enough. Eldon Metzger broke through a snow bridge over a crevasse but got out safely. Midafternoon found us again pitching our tents at Camp 1. In addition, a new large tent was waiting there to be tested. After a big meal, we had the best sleep of the trip.

The next day was essentially recreational skiing. We went back part way to pick up a cache and had a great ski run back down to camp.

On May 19, heavy winds took care of our final tent tests. All tents except the Everests fell apart in the wind. My biases about

Rainier summit disappearing in the fog

that tent were correct. The afternoon was spent packing loads for the return to base.

May 20 was our last day. The air was clear; the wind was down. Porters arrived at 8:00 A.M. I radioed to Paradise that we were leaving at 9:45 A.M. Before noon we were shuffling through sloppy spring snow to shake Colonel Rolfe's hand.

As we looked around, we had Rip Van Winkle syndrome. The changes in two weeks were impressive. The mountainside was now overrun with skiers camouflaged in white parkas and trousers. A close look at the garments revealed that the inner side of the outer garments had the standard army O.D. (olive drab) color for summer camouflage. The Mountain and Winter Warfare Board was working well.

Partial collapse of snow bridge reveals crevasse

Porters at Camp Muir ready to help on descent

The 87th Regiment was filling up. There were rumors of moving to a larger training site now being built in the mountains of Colorado and carrying the name Camp Hale. There our unit would expand to a division, the 10th Mountain Infantry Division, the first such unit in U.S. history. But what about officers to lead such a division? Up to this time commissioned officers leading the training program were the result of a happy coincidence of mountain men who had completed Reserve Officers' Training Camp (ROTC) or regular army officers who had enjoyed years of recreational skiing or mountaineering. But these were few. Most were already committed. It would take more than ten times as many officers to lead a division. How could they be trained?

There were a few regular army officers trying at this late date to learn alpine lore in a short course taught by noncommissioned experts. In the army, that kind of inverted rank is protocol-haywire. But worse, we were becoming aware that expert skiing and mountaineering cannot be achieved in a short course unless the candidate is an unusual teenager. The solution? Send our most mountain-worthy enlisted men to Ft. Benning, Georgia, for officer training and commissioning—making sure they are all returned to the mountain troops. This last feat would be almost as tradition-busting as having whippersnapper privates instructing commissioned officers.

The Japanese bombing of Dutch Harbor, June 3, 1942, and their insulting capture of the two U.S. islands, Attu and Kiska at the far end of the Aleutian chain, probably helped support the Ft. Benning solution. With a little local encouragement a few of our noncoms hit the trail to Ft. Benning. When they actually *were* returned with gold bars, the rest of us felt easier about taking the step.

Last of training at Paradise

Camp Hale, Colorado. Ready to take on 10th Mountain Division

In September 1942 I, too, applied to Ft. Benning. While I was gone the 87th, and all that went with it, moved to Camp Hale and the 10th Mountain Infantry Division started to grow. Very soon there were the 86th and 85th regiments.

On my way back to the outfit, a second lieutenant with a gold bar on each shoulder, I took a delay en route to marry a friend of long standing, Maynie Riggs of New York City. On Thanksgiving we were joined in the company of as many members of both families as could get a leave. Our temporary honeymoon consisted of a train ride to Colorado. We found a niche for Maynie in Glenwood Springs, among other military wives. I went on to Camp Hale, not far from the old mining town of Leadville. Camp Hale was located in a wide flat alpine valley bounded by high peaks. It was already full of barracks and other buildings. There were also lots of soldiers among the carpenters and builders. New to eye and thought was a large paddock of pack horses and mules.

I was assigned to a new arm of the division, the Mountain Training Group (MTG) with its headquarters, the Mountain Training Center (MTC) and its commander, Capt. John Woodward.

The mission of the Mountain Training Center was to make certain that every man in the 10th Mountain Infantry Division, from the cooks on down, knew how to cope with snow, ice, and mountains. We poured ourselves into that job. Most of our own newly commissioned officers were assigned to the line outfits, readying for war. Occasionally a detachment from the MTC would be sent out on special projects.

For instance, almost as soon as I reported in to MTC I was sent on a detachment with Billy Neidner to Camp McCoy, Wisconsin, to help winterize the Second Infantry Division. This

Maynie Riggs

outfit had been trained up to the hilt for combat. They were tough and ready—except they had been trained in the south and had never coped with bitter cold and deep snow. By the time they had completed this training they were tougher than ever.

I was then flown to Washington, D.C., to make a verbal report on a food test I had run for Captain Jackman. The test? My training squad and I lived on pemmican and water alone for the two weeks of the maneuver. Temperatures had ranged between -5 and -48°F. We lived and worked out of doors the whole time. The results? We gained a little weight. We were in excellent shape, felt fine, and were very tired of pemmican. Maynie caught up with me in Washington, D.C. We had a couple of uncomfortable days together. The hotel was way too hot for me and too cold for Maynie.

West Virginia was my next stop, where another detachment from MTC was conducting a rock climbing school for another division.

Early in May I was back at Camp Hale just in time to catch a radio report of the U.S. battle to drive the Japanese off the island of Attu. U.S. soldiers were successful, but the battle was bloody. The most unsettling to me was the report that U.S. soldiers had suffered almost as much from the weather as from the enemy. Why? Had the equipment not been given proper testing?

Things were happening fast, almost too fast to comprehend. Now a detachment of our 10th Mountain combat troops was going to be tested in actual combat—"Operation Cottage," the recovery of the island of Kiska from the Japanese. On August 15, 1943, the U.S. task force started the bombardment.

In this particular operation the Japanese apparently knew what was coming and when. Using fog and night for concealment, they spirited the last of their troops off the island a couple of days before the bombardment. The tundra of Kiska, some of our troops including a few of the 10th, and U.S. military pride suffered damage in that one-sided battle. Fog, excitement, and trigger-itch was responsible for the human losses.

By autumn 1943, things were fairly quiet but tense. America was mainly trying to hold Japan at bay in the South Pacific while the bulk of the troops worked with allies in Europe to settle our differences with Hitler first. The 10th Mountain Infantry had just about completed its mountain training and was ready for some battle practice before an overseas assignment. A detachment from MTC, including a First Lieutenant Bradley (with silver bars), was preparing for another assignment at Camp McCoy, Wisconsin; this time we would winterize the 76th

Division. Maynie moved to Madison, Wisconsin, to live with my parents near Camp McCoy. She was pregnant.

The Strange Case of a Survival Film

Some time before our winter training detachment pulled out for Wisconsin, a uniformed man I didn't know approached me rather secretively concerning a possible assignment for spring and summer of 1944. It seemed the Army Air Corp wanted a survival film for pilots downed in Alaska. The movie camp would probably be located 100 miles north of Juneau near Glacier Bay and would require eight to twelve of our enlisted instructors and perhaps another officer.

Having had experience in both professional photography and mountains, I had no misgivings about the assignment but I suggested that the gentleman go through channels to our commanding officer, Capt. John Woodward. I had no idea what John might already have planned for next summer. Just the barest flick of a smile crossed the poker face. He said, "Let's assume you'll do it. Keep it to yourself but be thinking about it and the men you'll need. If this works out you will be hearing about it next spring."

My mind was already leaping forward to a list of men. There were at least fifteen still left in MTC who were among the very best. Off in New Jersey was my brother, Steve, with the Signal Corps. He had been on the Dartmouth ski team, was a good mountaineer, and had already produced a training film for the

Maynie and Charles Jr.

Para-ski troops. Could he become involved? Yes, I thought about the proposition but only briefly. Very soon I was swallowed up in the winter training program for the 76th Division—and the advent of my firstborn, Charles Jr., who arrived most conveniently in my home town, Madison, Wisconsin, when I was on weekend leave there from Camp McCoy.

It was, of course, Charles Jr. who swept all thoughts of Glacier Bay from my mind. Spring 1944 came; the 76th Division thawed out and disappeared. I rented a small house in Leadville near Camp Hale and wrote to my wife, Maynie, to grab Charles Jr. and come to Colorado for some home making. That letter had hardly gone when Captain Woodward sent for me. "How'd you like to spend the summer in Alaska?" I gulped, remembered, took a deep breath, gagged a bit, and the C.O. added kindly, "Never mind, you're going anyway. Give me a list of ten enlisted men you'd like to go mountaineering with."

I met Maynie and Charles Jr. at the Denver train station with secret orders in my hand. Briefly (translated into civilian English):

RESTRICTED

June 1, 1944, The following named officers and enlisted men will proceed from this station to Seattle port of embarkation to arrive no later than June 5, reporting for shipment upon arrival . . . Temporary duty for approximately 60 days.

Capt. Gordon Stimson, 1st Lt. C. Bradley; S/Sgt. Geo. Gagnon, S/Sgt Robt. Niss, T/4 Robt. Brelsford, T/4 Fritz Ehrl, Cpl. Wm. Bowes, Cpl. Robt. French, T/5 Victor Gottschalk, T/5 Anton Matt, T/5 Horace Quick, T/5 Ernest Tapley.

RESTRICTED

Home making lasted two days. Maynie, a solid citizen if there ever was one, laughed at the irony. "See you in a couple of months," she said as she saw me off on the train. I was ready to eat, bones and all, a certain colonel who signed orders for the Second Army.

Well, as assignments go, this should be fun: good crew of mountaineers, Alaskan glaciers, only sixty days. I chatted with our gang and hinted at what we were headed for. We were all cheers. There was a question I did not voice: Why the sudden secrecy? We would not get our further orders until we got on board. When we did receive them, they were sealed and not to be opened until the ship was under way. The ship left dock at 2:00 A.M. while we were sound asleep.

Getting dressed for breakfast I looked out the porthole and got a real jolt. The west coast was over the horizon astern. Only a few snowy mountain summits were visible. This was *not* the inside channel to Glacier Bay. We were headed west across the Gulf of Alaska. In perturbation, Gordon Stimson and I ripped open our sealed orders:

SECRET SAILING LIST
EN ROUTE TO ARMAGEDDON

Stimson, Gordon. Capt. Inf.
Bradley, Charles C. 1st Lt. Inf.
(ten enlisted men)
Report to base commander for further orders

SECRET

Armageddon? A biblical battleground? Gotta be a code name. What's going on? Where are we headed? Avoiding our enlisted men like a plague, I prowled the ship looking for someone who knew Armageddon. It turned out that there was an officer who was returning to Armageddon from leave. "Armageddon? That's Dutch Harbor, Unalaska Island in the Aleutian Chain."

It was beginning to look as though the survival film might be out. But what was in? We finally had to tell the enlisted men. They howled, they screamed, they used impolite language. Some may have wept. A few in the group had helped fight the battle of Kiska. The rest had heard plenty about the Aleutians, the Home of Hell and Misery for planet Earth.

The Gang

The American G.I. in wartime does not have many unlimited prerogatives, but "bitching" is a well-used wide-open door. It probably helps relieve the tensions that arise from the abnormal life he is forced to live and the lack of control over his own future. It was a continuous surprise to me how little bitching was employed by our MTG detachment. After the initial chill from the discovery that we were headed for the Aleutians, our gang was once more leaning forward as we slid toward the new mystery assignment.

Capt. Gordon "Gordy" Stimson was a tall lean Californian from Los Angeles. His business was mortgage and loan but his hobby was camping in the Sierras. As an officer he was calm and firm, never an irritated word or wild burst of anger. He could afford that. At 6'4" he looked down on the world with a wider vista than most. If you were around Gordy long enough you saw a gentle person with deep concern for others, especially the enlisted men under his control.

Bob Niss was our staff sergeant. Prior to the war he had been a Milwaukee furniture dealer who enjoyed skiing. Bob was stocky, powerful and had a gorgeous blond moustache that he kept twisted with the help of Wiessner's Wonder Red ski wax. He also had an infectious belly laugh, especially when faced with some outrageous, insoluble incongruity. Having been

The Gang: L to R, Victor Gottschalk, Har Quick, Bob Brelsford, Gordy Stimson, Tap Tapley, Toni Matt, Bob French [in front of Toni, kneeling], George Gagnon, Bob Niss, Bill Bowes, and Fritz Ehrl

through the Battle of Kiska he was one of those who had a pretty clear view of the terrain and environment ahead of us.

The name, Sgt. Anton Matt, is not nearly as well known as his other name, Toni Matt, Austrian-American Olympic downhill skier, most famous in our gang for having been the first person with legs powerful enough and steady enough to schuss straight down the headwall of Tuckerman's Ravine on Mt. Washington. Toni was as much at home on a glacier or rock face as he was on skis. In our group he took on additional fame for his accuracy with a 60-mm mortar, hand held between his knees without tripod or base plate. Toni was the sort of quiet modest guy you put a lot of trust in.

When Horace "Har" Quick joined the Mountain Training Group at Camp Hale he and my brother Bill developed an unusual version of "Mumblety-Peg" consisting of taking turns throwing knives at each other's feet. The thrower lost if his knife didn't stick in the floor boards. The throwee lost if he didn't get his foot out of the way in time. Often both men won but there came that day when Bill lost, including a small piece of his big toe. Har had worked for the U.S. Fish and Wildlife Service in Colorado. He was a homemade naturalist who just plain loved the out-of-doors and knew how to get along in it. He was picked for the survival film especially because of his knowledge of wild plants and animals as emergency food. Sadly he became our first casualty in the Aleutians.

George Gagnon, who had been a back-country guide and skier from Maine, was famous with us for his ingenious improvisations when things went wrong. "Field Expedients" is what the army called them. His motto was "fix it or make do" and he always behaved as though there was no such thing as cold. To match his Maine accent he had a broad, slaunchwise grin, startling at first because of two gleaming symmetrically placed gold teeth. George was definitely one of those our detachment could not do without. He became our second casualty.

Bill Bowes was a mountain skier from Oregon. He first found fame in our group when he leaned out and grabbed our C.O., who was just teetering past the balance point on the edge of a seventy-foot cliff. Later Bob acquired additional merit during a sham battle where, in the thick of the morning fog, he lobbed his first 81-mm mortar shell right into the lap of "the enemy" ensconced high on a ridge.

Ernest Tapley of Massachusetts, part Native American, was one of our best all-around woodsmen and mountaineers. He was a crack shot and never known to tire.

Victor Gottschalk had been a mountain guide in the Alps and a ski instructor at Sun Valley. Bob Brelsford was a mountaineering instructor from California. Bob French and Fritz Ehrl were quiet but very competent mountain men and excellent teachers.

This whole gang had been carefully hand picked to help us do the survival film. The laugh is that faced with an unknown assignment in unknown territory we would have picked the same crew. So I had no qualms about the mystery of Armageddon, just curiosity. Glancing at our gang, I thought I saw something that looked suspiciously like eagerness.

Armageddon Ho!

The Gulf of Alaska is a place where the uncertainties of tomorrow are easily lost in the beauty and excitement of today. It was a new world to me. First came the whales—lots of them. In my whole life before I had seen three. Now there were hundreds. It is hard to think of these ponderous giants as frolicking. But there they were. Their hydrobatics stunned me. They spouted. They rolled. They slapped the water surface with their flukes, rivaling a cannon's roar. They leaped vertically almost clear of the water and then fell back with a splash that would have wet down our steamer.

Then there were the albatrosses that had the ability to use the updraft from wave crests to avoid flapping their wings. Gliding from wave crest to wave crest they kept pace with our ship mile after mile with time out for feeding. As I looked at our ship's funnel belching black smoke and felt the throb of the engine, the albatrosses seemed the absolute ultimate in energy conservation.

On our third night out from Seattle we had another type of diversion from the worries of tomorrow. About 10:00 P.M. there was a sudden sharp order over the loud speakers. "Attention! All lights out immediately. Repeat—all lights out. Put on your life jackets, report to the boat deck and remain quiet. That is all." The ship immediately changed to an irregular serpentine course. It bored through the black darkness, heaving and listing with each sharp turn. After some time in this blind world of sound and motion, the submarine alert was lifted. Whether the threat was real or an unadvertised dry run we were never told. But it certainly was a jazzy reminder that somewhere out there, among the whales and albatrosses, a world war was in progress and we were part of it. Probably the threat was real. The next day, Tokyo Rose's sexy radio voice jabbed us with, "Well, I understand that you guys on SE 2708 had some excitement last night. Don't despair. There'll be more."

Our first landfall on the voyage to Armageddon came on the far side of the Gulf of Alaska, 1,600 miles from Seattle. The island of Kodiak is famous for its giant bears, roaring glacial streams, rugged mountains, and beautiful harbor. To me it is also famous for a four-foot-thick blanket of volcanic ash donated in 1912 by Mt. Katmai, 100 miles away. The ash blanket, now generally well covered by vegetation, was still an important part of the landscape after thirty-two years.

We had a few hours of shore leave in the little town of Kodiak where the frontier foreground contrasted sharply with the pristine background. It was Saturday evening with the considerable daylight of subarctic June. House lights were bright. Voices, music and the crash of dancing boots leaped out from all the cracks. The streets were jammed and the most common sight was a sailor being held approximately vertical by two or three other sailors, or a G.I. being escorted somewhere by the military police. Out at the edge of town there was a long, silent, widely spaced line of males leading to the door of a small home. Every few minutes the line would move forward one notch.

As our ship pulled away from Kodiak, the discordant foreground faded and softened. Finally there remained only the town lights reflected on the water while the blue-gray silence of the snowy peaks in twilight quietly took over.

From Kodiak on, we began to see islands. Except for the occasional blast of sunlight through a hole in the cloud deck, the scene was a gray and blue wash in a variety of shades but always gray and blue. But there was magic in the changes. A dark rain squall would move by, then with a touch of the wand there was a mountainous island quite close, its snowy summit lost in the clouds. You could see the big rollers exploding up the cliffs where there were also cascades of water from melting snow fields above. In a few minutes that island would vanish in a fog bank and be replaced by a couple of tiny islets looking calm and peaceful. Then a squall of mixed rain and snow would drive us toward the cabins and when it passed the sea was empty. The changing scene was hypnotic, unbelievable.

When the sun did break through, it was a spotlight that turned the sea a deep rich blue while an island suddenly became clothed, down to the beach, in bright green tundra, capped in crystal white. The lushness of the vegetation was obvious in sunlight. The usual blue and gray colors had me picturing the islands as forbidding lifeless outcrops of volcanic rock. Now I couldn't wait to get ashore and start prowling around.

Along with the islands, we began to see more marine life. Floating patches of kelp, seals, more whales, even an occasional sea otter—and thousands, yes millions of birds flying around in massive flocks or resting on the water in acre-sized rafts that undulated like a magic carpet on the huge Pacific swells.

One adventure with these birds I record here just in case it carries some cryptic message for the military.

Puffins! What an unlikely product of evolution is a puffin. Decorated to the hilt in wild and garish colors, a face that would discourage even a mother puffin (it was all beak), a voice that scorns music, a body shape that scorns the laws of aerodynamics. I met my first puffin here floating on the ocean in a mass of his buddies that extended almost to the horizon. At that moment I didn't know that this bird was not only a puffin but a leader of puffins, a bird worth watching.

Our ship was plowing along past an island that lay a couple of miles off our right side. The endless raft of puffins was on our left. With no malice, I'm sure, our captain had interjected the ship between the puffins and the island where they nested. My puffin, always alert, recognized the threat, said something to his buddies at the top of his lungs, and took off, flying diagonally across the bow of the ship, making a beeline for home. A few of his buddies gave tongue and followed their leader across the bow of the ship, heading for the island. Several more puffins got the message out, lifted off, and followed. By now the noise of agitated puffins made your head ache. Hundreds and then thousands of puffins thrashed free of the water, following the others storming around the bow of the ship and off toward home.

At the end of half an hour (I mean it) there were still panicked puffins beating their way around the bow of the steamer on the trail of their buddies. The catch is that by this time the island they were heading for was far, far behind. These birds were now flying twenty miles out of their way just to get around the bow of the ship.

The next morning, 600 miles from Kodiak, we woke up in the Aleutian Islands. Specifically we were in the process of docking at—well—"Armageddon," if you must know, or *sotto voce*, Dutch Harbor, Unalaska Island. From Kodiak our course had been changed from west to southwest, paralleling the huge volcanic welt on the earth's crust that makes up the Alaska Peninsula before most of the welt goes submarine, leaving visible only the volcano tops known as the Aleutian Islands. Unalaska is the second major island off the end of the peninsula. The island is linear, with a big head to the northeast tapering to a tail southwest. Dutch Harbor is at the head and beautifully protected from storms. Immediately to the north is a whaleback of a mountain named Ballyhoo, by that wild Irish author Jack London, or so we were told. To the west and south is Mt. Makushin, Unalaska's slumbering volcano with a glacial cap and a plume of vapor thundering like a blast furnace out of a blue hole in the top. Out in Unalaska Bay, looking us in the eye to remind us again of the war, was the rusting hull of a steamer that was sunk during the Japanese attack, almost exactly two years previously. The wreck looked forgotten and much older than that.

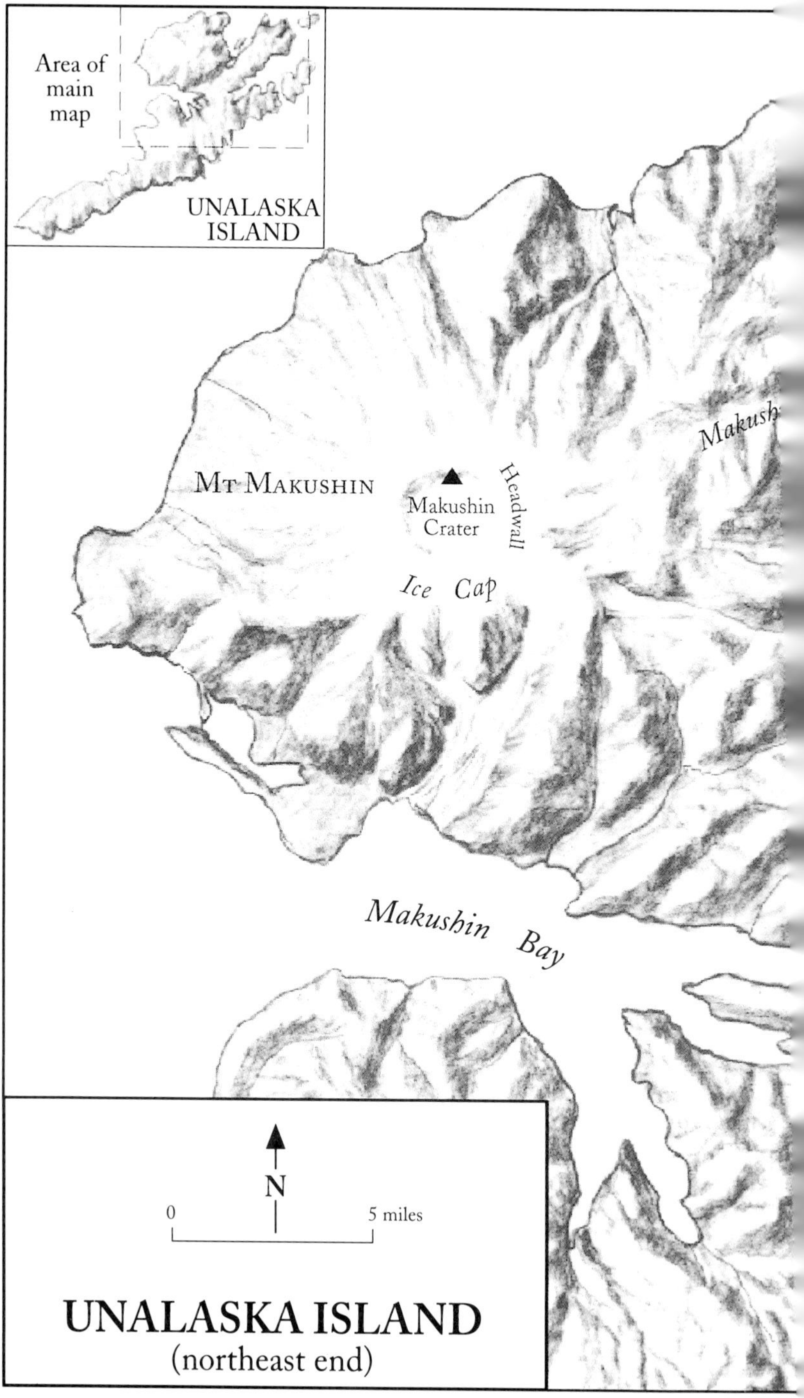

Area of
main
map
UNALASKA
ISLAND
MT MAKUSHIN
Makushin
Crater
Headwall
Ice Cap
Makushin Bay
N
0
5 miles
UNALASKA ISLAND
(northeast end)

Molenaar Landform Maps
BERING SEA
Unalaska Bay
Mt Ballyhoo
Airstrip
Dutch Harbor
Mt Newhall
Unalaska
Fort Mears
Beaver Inlet
PACIFIC OCEAN

Reminder of bombing at Dutch Harbor

As we stepped off onto the dock, the production of an Army Air Corps survival film vanished forever without a trace. There, waiting to greet us was a certain Maj. Frank Forrest, Commanding Officer of the North Pacific Combat School—to be.

The C.O. and His Baby

There is no way of avoiding first impressions, especially when meeting a person you have never even heard of and who is about to exercise considerable control over your life. My first impression of Maj. Frank Forrest was that he seemed pretty young to be a major. On the other hand he had an intensity that showed in his eyes and the way he moved. "A restless doer and a man with a purpose," I thought. "Best we get braced for action." He also smiled and laughed quite readily (I always worry about people who can't laugh) and he seemed friendly enough for a commanding officer.

Frank had graduated with a lieutenant's commission from West Point in 1939 and joined the 37th Infantry in Oregon. Shortly thereafter the 37th was moved to Fort Mears, the army base for Unalaska. For two and a half years Frank served there and was present when the Japanese bombed the place on June 4, 1942. In the autumn of 1943 he was released to participate in some Alaskan winter maneuvers scheduled for January to March 1944. Immediately after that experience he was invited by the Canadian Army to attend a mountain warfare school at Prince George, Canada, during the month of April. These two experiences set him thinking about the possibility of a mountain warfare school in the Aleutians that could prepare ground troops to carry the war back to the Japanese on Paramushiro in the northern Kuril Islands.

Paramushiro is one of the largest islands in the Kuril chain, Japan's twin sister to the Aleutian chain. Paramushiro's relationship to the Kamchatka Peninsula is very similar to Unalaska's relationship to the Alaska Peninsula. This is true geographically, geologically, and climatologically. It is not true politically. In 1944 the Kuril Islands were Japanese while the Kamchatka Peninsula was in the hands of one of their enemies, the Soviets.

Paramushiro supported Japan's biggest military base in the Kurils. They were expanding it at a feverish rate—and well they might. Paramushiro was less than a hundred miles from the USSR and only 650 miles from USA territory. Were they planning another attack on Alaska or were they digging in against an American-Soviet pincer movement from the north? In any case, from our standpoint no more perfect training ground for Kuril warfare exists than the Aleutian Islands—and, let us remember, vice versa. The Japanese were able to attack Dutch Harbor and were difficult to dislodge from Attu and Kiska precisely because they had trained in the Kurils.

Frank fired off his detailed five-page proposal to the Alaskan Department on 11 May 1944. Ten days later he received the following one-page order over Lt. Gen. Simon Bolivar Buckner's signature. In part:

SECRET

Gen. Order	**Headquarters Alaska Dept.**
No. 96	**21 May, 1944**

Effective this date, North Pacific Combat School is established at Ft. Mears, Unalaska with the allotted strength of 6 officers and 82 enlisted men who will constitute the permanent school staff.

The mission of NPCS will be to develop and conduct courses of instruction in amphibious, mountain and "muskeg" combat techniques to infantry units of this dept.

Major Frank G. Forrest is designated as Commandant of NPCS and will be responsible directly to the commanding general, Alaskan Dept.

SECRET

General Buckner's order had modified and greatly shortened Major Forrest's proposal. The mission was much less specific in terms of application and more specific in certain aspects of the curriculum. (What in the world is "muskeg" combat?) But quite clearly Lt. Gen. Simon Bolivar Buckner had said "yes" emphatically, wasting neither words nor time.

Back in 1943 the Joint Chiefs of Staff had ordered General Buckner and Admiral Thomas C. Kincaid to prepare detailed plans for the invasion of Paramushiro to be used only if Russia could be persuaded to join the party. Target date was June 1, 1944. It seems likely that General Buckner's instant positive response to Major Forrest's proposal was related to this assignment. The major promptly got off a request for assistance from the 10th Mountain Division at Camp Hale, which ultimately led to our Mountain Training Group detachment.

Presumably it was part of the standard smoke screen accompanying the word "secret" that, as one of the junior officers, I saw none of these documents.

In any case Maj. Frank G. Forrest was now C.O. and had his baby in hand. What next?

Maynie's Bull's Eye

Major Forrest showed us to our quarters at Ft. Mears. Gordon Stimson and I were assigned to a snug little Yakutat hut. Our enlisted men were housed together in a Quonset hut. Other members of the school staff were already on hand and more were arriving. We were introduced to Capt. Martin Krause, a lawyer from Wisconsin, and Lt. Harry Hitchcock, a Pennsylvania forester from Georgia. These two officers had arrived with the 58th Infantry sent to reinforce Dutch Harbor after the Japanese bombing. They became acquainted with Major Forrest at that time. When the major returned in spring of 1944 with his orders from General Buckner, Captain Krause and Lieutenant Hitchcock volunteered for NPCS. They were living in another Yakutat hut near ours.

Major Forrest left us with the suggestion that we get settled, and for the rest of the afternoon stroll around, getting acquainted with the lay of the land and a feel for the community. "We'll have an officers' meeting at 8:00 tomorrow morning. See you then."

The weather that first day was cool and sunny with white puffy low-hanging clouds moving across the mountain faces. It took us a few days to discover that this was weather especially reserved for newcomers. Good weather is not unheard of in the Aleutians in June, but—well—tomorrow would be different. It was always different tomorrow. Sometimes even today. In the meantime we enjoyed the beauty of the place.

Dutch Harbor itself is an embayment in Amaknak Island at the south end of Unalaska Bay. The island with the naval station is just offshore from Unalaska Village but connected to it

Dutch Harbor at Unalaska Village, Unalaska

by a short ferry ride. Its highest point, with an airstrip carved into its base, is Mt. Ballyhoo. Unalaska village, surrounded by Ft. Mears, is nestled into the mouth of a wide U-shaped stream valley backed by rounded grassy hills and nearby mountains with perhaps 2,000 feet of relief. No trees. Farther back were the snow-covered peaks going up to 6,000 feet or more. From a little distance the nearby terrain looked like a huge well-tended golf course. Shortly we were to learn otherwise.

The village was a small cluster of houses, shacks, and sheds—weathered and gray. There was a feeling about it of stark function and human stubbornness as a substitute for opulence. I believe that Dutch Harbor had been a fishing village and whaling station prior to the advent of the military base which, by 1944, had expanded upstream from the village.

Right in the middle of town was a startling remnant of pre-American occupation, a church, looking completely out of place, sporting a bright red roof and two equally bright green onion-shaped domes in lieu of steeples. It was a thrill to have at least one reminder of how close we came to having Russia as co-occupant of the North American continent instead of having what would become the forty-ninth state of the Union.

I dashed back to our hut, got out my pad and the little box of watercolors Maynie gave me before we left. With no comment or identification I sent the sketch to Maynie that afternoon. It was one of my first and worst attempts at watercolor. Perhaps that is why the censors let it go through. Thereafter I often sent Maynie sketches instead of letters. [A portfolio of the author's watercolors follows page 107.]

This particular sketch, however, was special in another way. Before I left Camp Hale I worked out a code with Maynie that would let her know quite precisely where I was in Alaska. However, the assumption, based on the Air Corps survival film, was that we would be somewhere in southern Alaska. When we landed on Unalaska, the best I could do with the code was to let her know it wouldn't work. At least she would know where I wasn't. In a couple of weeks I got an innocent letter from Maynie telling me how my son was growing and how much she missed me, etc. Enclosed was a clipping from the *New York Times* which included an old pencil sketch by John Muir entitled "Oonalaska, Aleutian Islands," featuring the church. Done from a viewpoint opposite mine, it showed the knoll from which I made my sketch. It was a worse sketch than mine, which is probably why the censors let it through. Maynie did well to recognize the church. Muir's sketch shows a church somewhat different from mine, but Maynie, historian and archaeologist, had made a bull's eye.

John Muir's sketch of Unalaska including the Russian church

Up the hill from the Russian church was a cemetery that appeared to be connected to it historically. It was well furnished with wooden crosses, battered, weathered and tilted by Aleutian zephyrs. Nearly all were the double crosses of Russian Orthodox design, displaying also the slanting support for Christ's feet near the base. I sent a watercolor of the cemetery to Maynie so that she would know I knew she knew my whereabouts. [See portfolio, watercolors 1 and 3.]

The Assignment

The scene: Russian church, village of Unalaska. Four NPCS officers are having their first official meeting with the commandant. A storm outside is vibrating the venerable building.

Major Forrest: "The mission of the North Pacific Combat School is to train a group of instructors who will help prepare a task force to attack the Kuril Islands. For us this means mainly working with the mountain infantry arm of the task force that will be trying to capture and hold the high ground, and deal with an enemy who is already well trained and is probably expecting us.

"I want you to impress upon our enlisted men at the start the absolute necessity for secrecy. It is our necks and those of the instructors we train, as well as the task force. I have every expectation that all of us—all of us except the MTG detachment which is on loan for a couple of months; the rest of us will be absorbed into the task force after training is over. We'll be in the thick of the combat. Betrayal of the secret is betrayal of ourselves and our buddies. We must all take pains not to discuss the mission or activities outside the group. They should even avoid saying: 'Sorry, I can't tell you. It's a big secret!' When the conversation starts to focus too much, get vague, mumble, change the subject, or go to the bathroom. Naturally no hints should find a way into the mail. Speaking of which, all officers will have an active part in the censorship of enlisted mail. And you can expect to have your own mail censored. So behave accordingly.

"Are there any questions?"

First officer: "Yes. Is there a program or curriculum that will be a general guide for the instruction?"

Major Forrest: "Not at the moment. The development of the curriculum and a manual will be our first official assignment. However, since only a few of you have ever been in the Aleutian Islands I suspect that the first chore is for all of us to spend a couple of weeks assessing the situation and the terrain, learning as much as we can from the land and from each other before settling on a specific plan, finding special instructional sites, and drafting the manual.

"Horse sense suggests that a general curriculum sequence would be: First, survival; second, mobility; third, tactics. You can't even move around in this place unless you learn the art of survival. You will discover that is not a trivial matter. Don't be fooled by our June weather—especially yesterday's. And you can't fight a war here unless you know how to get through the mountains in a fog, cross the many roaring streams, land on boulder beaches in heavy surf, hide in a landscape without trees, etc. So I think the sequence of survival, mobility, and tactics is a logical framework on which to build the training.

"Any more questions?"

Second officer: "How many instructors are we to train and what is the approximate time frame to have the whole instructional cadre ready for the task force?"

Major Forrest: "The total strength of the school staff has not been settled and we have no time frame for training completion. We start with the five officers and twenty-odd enlisted men who are here and build our cadre from them as fast as we can. The way the Pacific war is progressing, we don't dare waste a day. Besides, we want to make the best use we can of the Mountain Training Group from the 10th Mountain Infantry. They'll be returning to Camp Hale in August."

The C.O. had left us with much to ponder and a feeling of urgency. Gordy Stimson and I walked back through a mixture of rain and fog riding on a forty-mile breeze. Our treasured two-ply mountain jackets (issued only to 10th Mountaineers!) were wet through by the time we entered the hut. It was a gentle reminder that educational topic 1, survival, in the Aleutians is

Mountain traning starts, Mt. Ballyhoo, background, Unalaska

mostly a matter of surviving the Aleutian weather, something most of us had yet to experience. The worst would come in November and December. Our detachment was scheduled to leave around the first of August. How in the world were we going to be effective as instructors in survival? What sort of clothing and shelter would the troops be issued? We hoped it would be something more suitable than mountain jackets, and something more suitable than what had been issued to the poor devils who fought the Battle of Attu, two years ago. From what we had read they were not only untrained for mountain warfare but were equipped for the temperate zone with G.I. standard clothing and leather footgear. They sustained huge casualties from the weather alone.

Cold weather per se was no problem to our 10th Mountain team any more. We had camped in -48°F in windy terrain—but we had been dry. Survival here was going to be quite different. We had a lot to learn ourselves before we could teach. We had become accustomed to self-training on Mt. Rainier, but it does take time. Furthermore, experience had taught us not to assume that the right kind of clothing, shelter and other equipment was already on hand for issue. If it was not, that meant hasty experiment and design, contact with the Office of Quartermaster General (OQMG), Washington, D.C., for help in getting samples made up. Then we would have to give them a good field test with reports back to OQMG for modification. That would take months and we would be long gone back to Camp Hale by then. How the devil was our detachment going to be useful to NPCS?

The worry about our own ignorance was tempered by the knowledge that our C.O. had spent a lot of time in the Aleutians and that there were others coming in daily to join the enlisted force who knew something about survival here. We were about to meet Ivar Skarland, a 65-year-old Norwegian anthropologist from the University of Alaska, Lloyd Ahvakana, a young Eskimo from Point Barrow, and Kakik, an Aleut who had been evacuated early in the war, with the remnants of his colony, from the islands to the mainland. Also arriving were some remnants of the Alaskan scouts who had patrolled the immense coastline and innumerable islands for information on the location and movement of Japanese troops immediately after the bombing of Dutch Harbor. If ever there were survival experts, these were they.

History occasionally provides a comforting perspective. Before the arrival of the early Russian fur traders, there was a

Ivar Skarland

time when as many as 16,000 Aleuts had called these islands home. They had occupied them for thousands of years. Obviously they had worked out the first two of our problems, survival and mobility. On the third problem, combat tactics, history is a little unsettling. The Aleuts were, in general, a cooperative people who were almost completely wiped out by the Russian fur traders.

Kakik

First Look at Mobility

Rising steeply up out of Dutch Harbor are the green foothills where we started our inspection of Aleutian terrain for lessons to be learned relative to survival, mobility, and conduct of a war. Landscape is often the object of close scrutiny by the eyes of science, engineering, and art. The civilian, even the civilian mountaineer, drawn suddenly into warfare may have to change drastically his habits of landscape perception in order to survive. This was the first step in our assignment: to see, to learn and then to teach how to use the Aleutian landscape to advantage in combat—and to avoid the military traps that lurk therein. Lessons would come, but not necessarily in the prescribed logic of the education program. All we could do was make notes on items of military significance as they revealed themselves to us.

In the waves of fog and drizzle that alternately opened and closed the vistas ahead this day it was the mystery and beauty, not the war with Japan, that lifted our feet up the hillside. The lush vegetation was called "tundra" by those of our group who were familiar with the Aleutians. Permafrost is not a feature of the Aleutians where the temperature, modified by the ocean currents, rarely gets very far below freezing. The ground tends to be hummocky and a little boggy even on steep hillsides. The ground cover is a mat of tall coarse grasses and sedges and, at this time of year, a profusion of alpine and subalpine flowers are in bloom.

With a new issue of rain jackets, rain pants and shoepacks as footgear we were fairly well protected from the water-saturated atmosphere and ground cover. In terms of mobility we could not avoid noting that the hummocks and vegetation absorbed a great deal of the energy going into forward motion. The distant illusion of the well-groomed hillside was gone. One of the more serious illusions produced by the distant view of steep mountain slopes was that since they were clothed in green, ascent was just a walk-up. We were to find out in due time that because of the green cover, ascent was often very hazardous or impossible for a foot soldier loaded with combat and survival gear.

Another problem in mobility that took considerable study was the all too frequent steep-sided V-shaped gorges, cut through

Unalaska, first flowers of spring

slope-rubble by a rip-snorting stream lying in wait at the bottom. It took a nerve-wracking amount of time for a platoon of men to work their way down the slope without killing each other with rolling boulders, getting across the stream without losing their footing, and up the other side still intact. It was nerve wracking because in combat, a large group of distracted soldiers packed into a gorge could become the victims of a massacre. Over the days ahead we timed the crews as they tried various arrays of rope for rappelling down the slopes side by side, rope handrails across the stream, and ropes to speed the climb out. We even set up Tyrolean traverses—taut ropes spanning the chasm for moving gear and/or men directly across from rim to rim.

Those assists sped up the process considerably, but the time spent in crossing was still such that it was preferable to avoid

Rappelling into gorge, Unalaska

the chasms if at all possible. This led in turn to the idea that the ridges were the way. We were back to the military axiom: "take and hold the high ground"—doubly important in the mountains and doubly difficult to achieve.

Tyrolean traverse over gorge,
Sergeant Bob Niss, Unalaska

COVER, CONCEALMENT, AND *CORVUS*

As mentioned earlier, one of the many difficulties in conducting a war in the Aleutians is the absence of trees and brush for cover and concealment. The wide-open green hillsides and snowy mountain sides not only advertise the presence of man, but they clearly reveal his tracks and those of his vehicles. For all the rugged appearance of that coarse vegetation and the labor-intensive chore of walking through it, the tundra is amazingly sensitive to disturbances. We had already noted on the edge of Ft. Mears a naked patch in the tundra where the ground cover had been borrowed to camouflage a Quonset hut.

That was three years ago and there was no evidence of new growth healing the scar. None. Later, in our ascent of Mt. Makushin we followed a trail in the tundra made by a single party of climbers that included Major Forrest three years before. We could see it for miles ahead of us. Clearly we would have to give these matters some military consideration.

Two obvious thoughts for concealment in the Aleutians are night and fog. Night is a feature you can count on taking place regularly. Night exercises, however, would have to wait until we were all a lot more familiar with the terrain, and the instructional team had been checked out individually on their nocturnal abilities. Fog would have to be used opportunistically—with one hand on the "Plan B" button for that moment when the fog suddenly disappeared. But we could check out the possibilities of fog any foggy day.

We didn't have to wait very long for the next foggy day. Our instructional team was divided into two patrols of about twelve each. There were two officers with each patrol. One was commander, the other was an impartial observer who watched, made notes, and remained silent.

Out there in the fog south of Dutch Harbor was a spur of Mt. Newhall. We had often seen it but had never been there. The ridge line itself was roughly horizontal at an elevation of about 2,000 feet. We climbed to a knoll and faced the invisible ridge. One team moved off to the right for about a mile. The other did the same to the left. Almost from the first step the two teams had lost contact. Now separated by about two miles, both teams climbed directly up the slope to the ridge, where they faced each other and moved cautiously forward.

The substance of the exercise was to try to detect the other team first and set up an entrapment. Both teams were required

Cover in concealment on Mt. Newhall, Unalaska

to press forward continuously until contact was made. For realism both were attired as combat patrols, armed with helmets, M-1 rifles, bayonets, ammunition belts, and dummy hand grenades. I was observer for one patrol with Lt. Harry Hitchcock as commander.

The climb up the slope was a lesson in itself. The clanking of metal gear and the sound of rolling rocks were probably not audible two miles away but would have been nerve wracking for a patrol searching for a real enemy in the fog. We would have to pad the gear and learn to walk the Aleutian slopes with much greater precision before we would be ready to teach anyone about tactical mobility.

On top of the ridge the going proved to be quite easy. The humps often showed exposed bedrock while the saddles tended to be grassy. Lieutenant Hitchcock started with two points (leaders), one on each side of the ridge so as to be less visible but able to spot a foggy silhouette on the crest. Early on he gave that up because the hillside footing was bad and rock noises too great. The patrol now moved in single file, strung out to minimum visual contact through the line. This involved closing and expanding with the thickening and thinning of the fog. At one time we were panicked by a wide open hole in the fog, complete with bright sunshine. The patrol halted and hunkered down, making like a group of large geological specimens. The hole was not large enough to expose the enemy and in a twinkling the fog shut down again—but not before we had had a gorgeous view across the cloud deck to the summit of Mt. Makushin with its plume of steam streaming out down wind. Some day we would have to climb it.

Not very long after the sunshine scare, our point began to catch, within the erratic rumbles of the wind, a mumble of voices in low conversation. He moved in a little closer to make sure and then raised his hand. We all stopped moving forward and sneaked alternately off the crest. What in the devil was going on? Was the other patrol almost criminally careless or were the voices bait for a trap? Our own patrol with its men distributed on each side of the crest were now in a kind of open pincer formation. We moved carefully forward, straining to see into the swirling fog.

Pretty soon our points raised their hands to signal a halt. At the same time we heard a burst of laughter, sounding almost within visual distance. There as we waited, all tense, for the fog to thin, we heard all-out belly laughter. Completely mystified now, we waited and waited. A sudden thinning of the fog gave us a fast glimpse ahead and then shut down again. What we had seen in that flash was what appeared to be a group of four to six people on a sloping patch of old snow. One was sliding down the patch on his fanny, the others, probably drunk, were watching and laughing hilariously. Obviously our buddies had blown the game and had taken up late winter recreation. We cautiously moved forward for the next look. This could be a very sophisticated trap.

The next look was very clear and astounded us almost into a state of shock. The fog had distorted our sense of distance and details of outline. We were watching six ravens. Five were standing in a row down the fall line of the snow slope making a variety of conversation-like noises and calling—Haw! Haw! Haw!—as they watched one of their number slide down the slope. The bird was dragging its tail feathers, feet forward, wings partially spread for lateral stability. As he picked up speed he became airborne, circled the updraft and landed with the spectator group to watch another raven try a ride.

The big black birds were apparently so occupied that they hadn't spotted the twelve extra spectators. We remained quiet, watching this amazing scene fade in and out of the streaming fog. Pretty soon repressed snorts and squeaks were oozing out of the patrol. Finally we caved in and joined the ravens in all-out belly laughter—at which they vanished—zap! In the science of animal behavior we are sternly warned against viewing such antics with an anthropomorphic bias. In this test we probably all failed. How else would one interpret sliding down a snow bank except for fun? There was no other visible reward. What were the gurgles and calls if not sounds of enjoyment?

At risk of disappointing the military scientists among my readers, I have to admit that my memory of our first exercise in the tactical use of fog ends here. For the life of me I cannot remember even meeting the other patrol, nor returning to Ft. Mears, nor filing any report with Major Forrest. All that really sticks in my mind is my first meeting with *Corvus corax*, the Northern Raven, who would jazz up our lives again and again before V-J Day.

Mobility in Eden

June and July in the Aleutians is a time of floral extravagance, so breathtakingly beautiful that it was difficult to keep the mind on such urgent matters as survival, mobility, and tactics. My grandfather and my father were both excellent amateur botanists, but until Unalaska I had not been bitten by the bug of identification. Now, however, I was feeling the urge to know the names and faces.

Without stretching things too much I could point out that in the matter of survival, some of these plants or their fruits were edible. In fact we had been issued a mimeograph pamphlet on emergency foods in the Aleutians that identified the local edible plants. But after trying, for instance, the boiled starchy root of the black-blossomed Kamchatka Lily, my gut reaction was to have my emergency near the coast where a shore dinner of fresh fish, shrimp, mussels, and clams was easily harvested and prepared. It also helped me to forget the durable bitterness of the lily root. But I'll never forget the only black blossom I've ever seen. In short, my desire to learn something about the flowers had less to do with gastronomy than the fact that they were there.

Unalaska had no flower book, but I had something better, T5g Horace "Har" Quick, naturalist for the MTC detachment. Long ago he had made friends with plants. With his help on identification, I began to sketch the flowers and learn their names. As time went by, my attention to floral detail increased and I added such correlative data as date of the sketch, altitude, etc., as their usefulness in identification or association became apparent. The activity was vastly absorbing, making the islands a more interesting and friendly place.

On this particularly beautiful day, as we strolled up the rounded back slope of a foothill that had a near-vertical cliff face on the far side, I made hasty sketches and notes about the flowers, even pressed a few small ones in my notebook. It was the perfect day for anything, such as not hurrying, looking at flowers, even rappelling. Our official purpose in being here was to check out the cliff as a possible site for advanced instruction in the art of the rappel. For the uninitiated, a rappel is a method for rapid descent on a rope without strain or rope burns and under complete control. It can be done badly and dangerously. So we started our students on walk-up slopes, increasing the pitch finally to vertical cliffs and overhangs as they demonstrated the ability. A student here would experience the difficulties associated with getting over the lip of an overhang and then the thrill of being suspended on a three-eighths-inch rope over a hundred or so feet of fresh air, and faced with the necessity of sliding down the rope without getting tangled or rolling out of the rappeller's hitch.

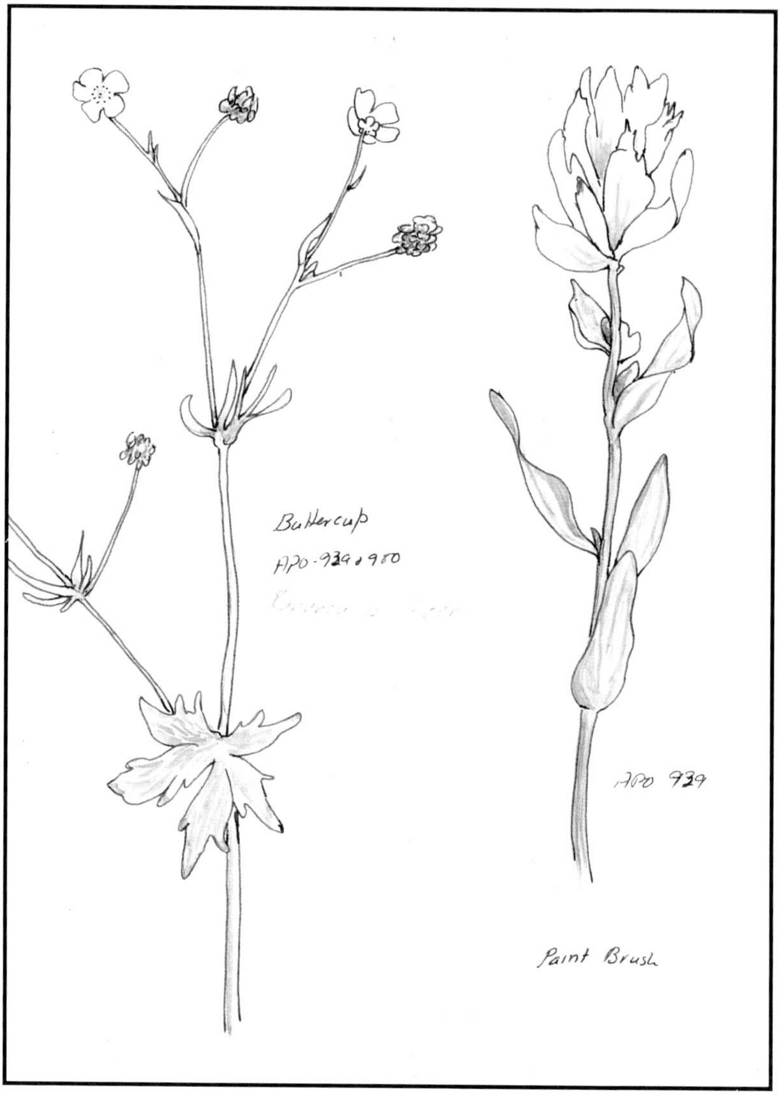

(left) Buttercup (Ranunculus sp.), *(right) Indian Paintbrush* (Castilleja unalaschensis)

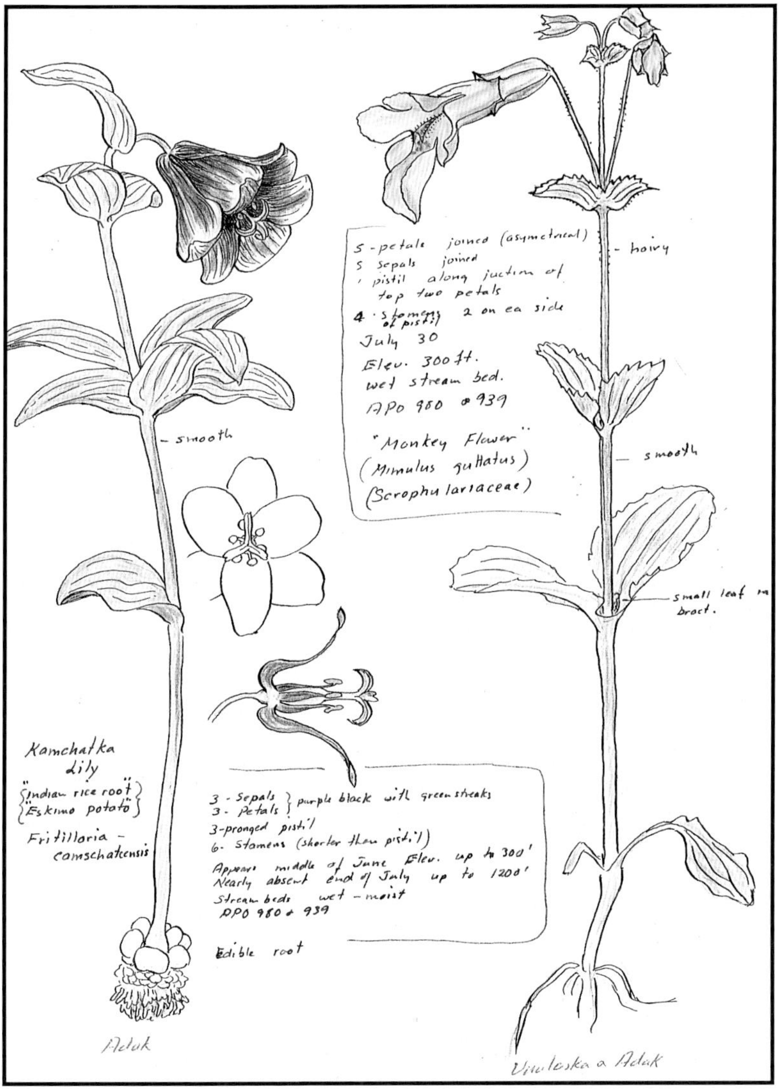

(left) Kamchatka Fritillary (Fritallaria camschatcensis), *(right) Yellow Monkey Flower* (Mimulus guttatus)

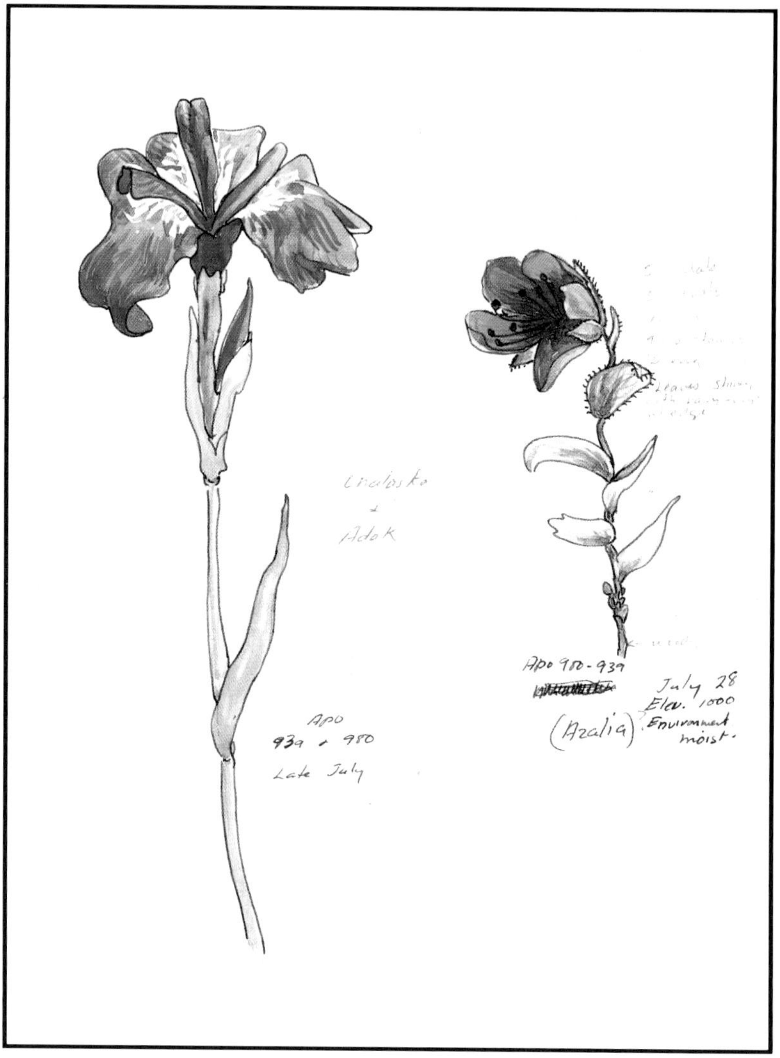

(left) Wild Flag (Iris setosa), *(right) Kamchatka Rhododendron* (Rhododendron camtschaticum)

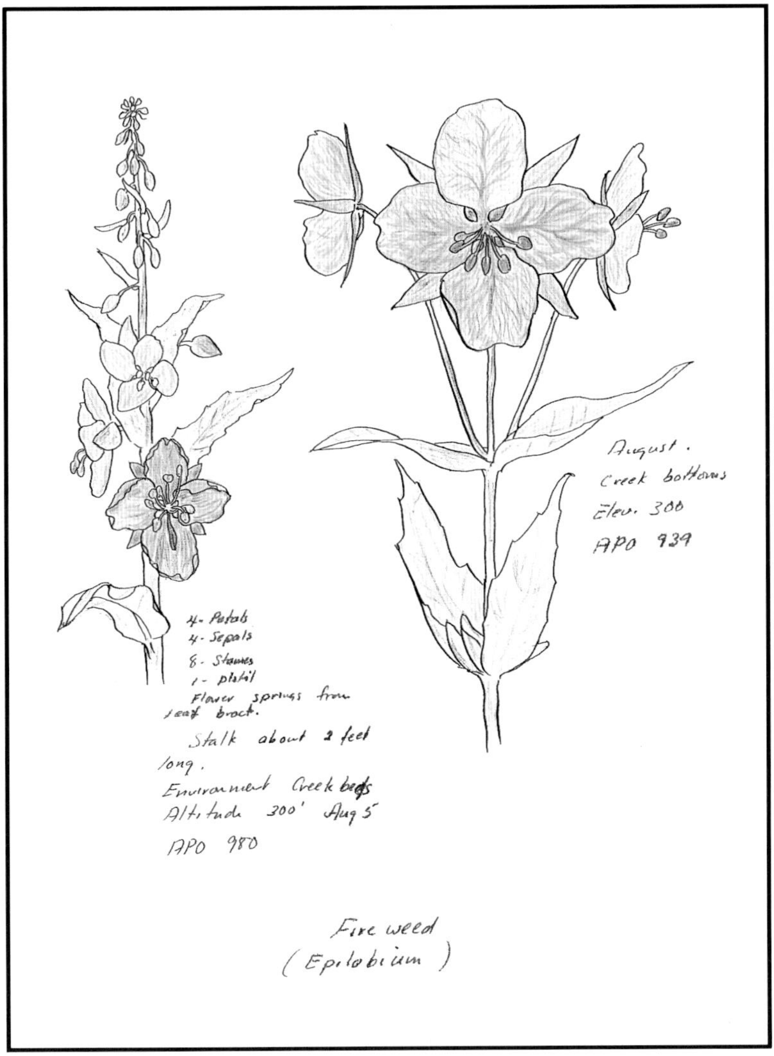

(left) Fireweed (Epilobium angustifolium), *(right) River Beauty* (Epilobium latifolium)

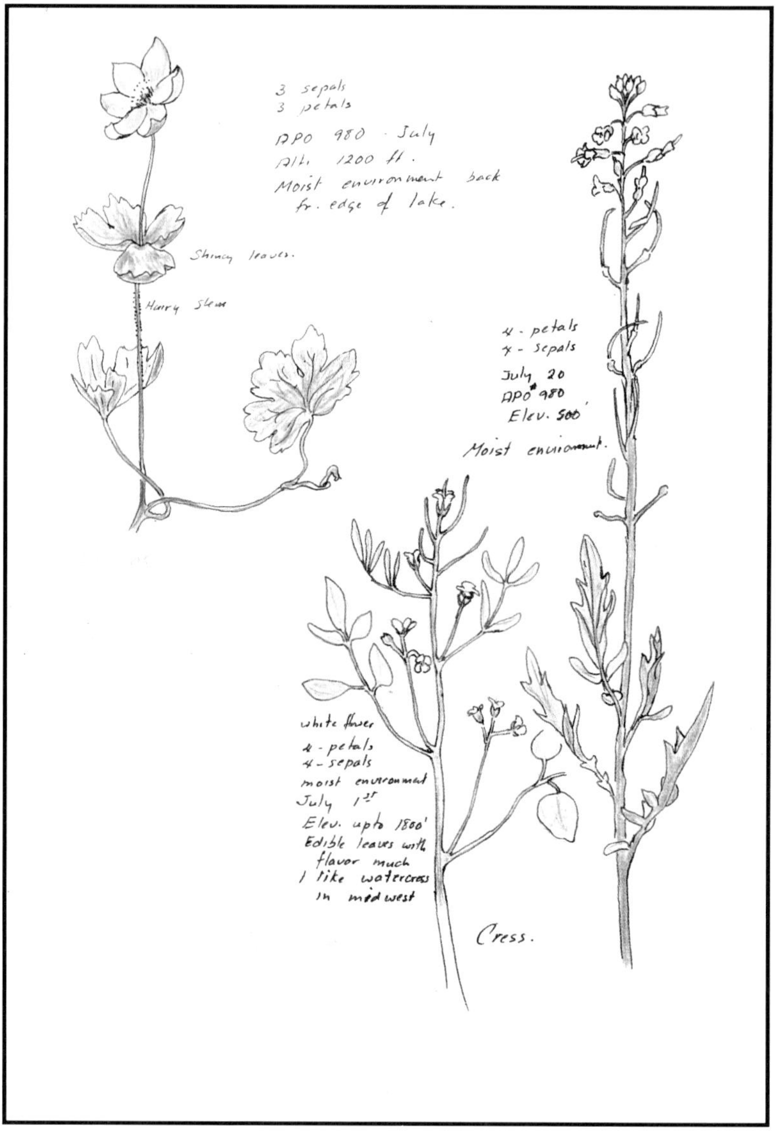

(left) Anemone (Anemone sp.), *(center) Bitter Cress* (Cardamine sp.), *(right) Mustard family* (Cruciferae sp.)

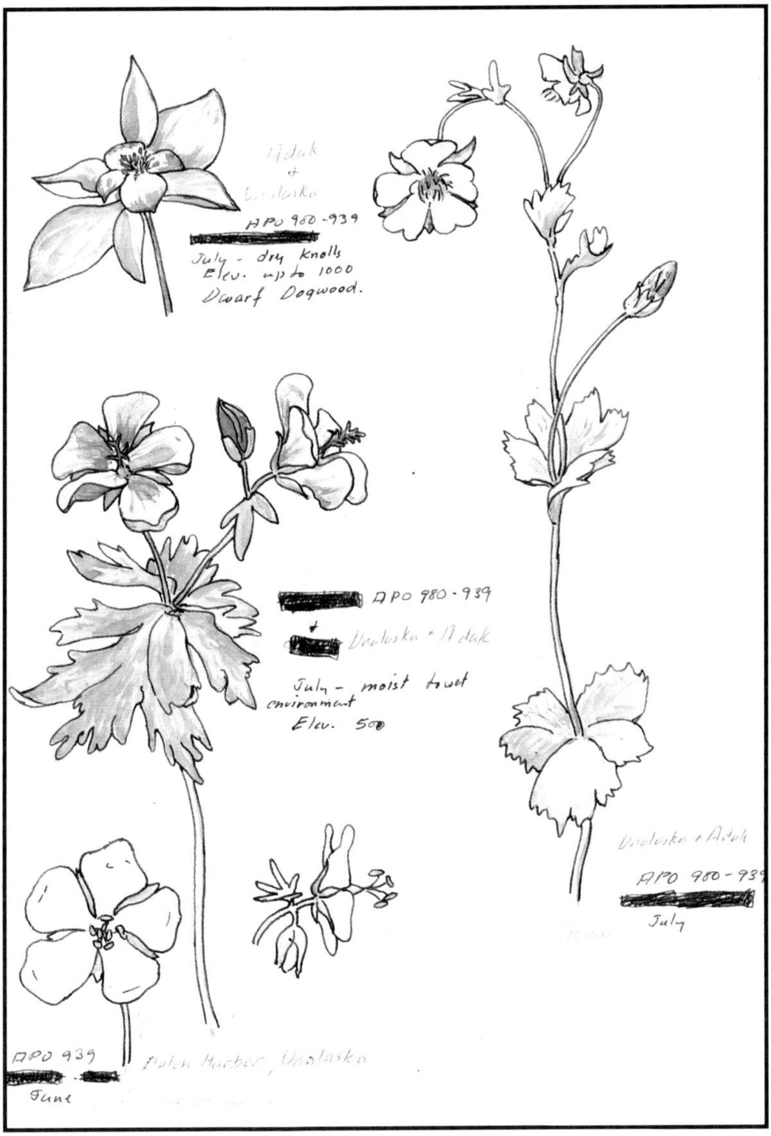

(left upper) Bunchberry (Cornus canadensis), *(left lower) Geranium* (Geranium erianthum), *(right) Avens* (Geum sp.)

Our party was the four junior officers responsible for conducting the education program—Stimson, Krause, Hitchcock, and Bradley. In this case, because I'd had a hundred or so more miles of rappelling than the others, I was leader for the day. I should say at this point that almost any of our enlisted men knew more about rappels than any of the officers, but they were on teaching duty elsewhere this day. We had already studied the cliff face with binoculars from several vantage points. Today we were going to study the cliff, face to face. First we would descend on a route that did not involve the overhang but would allow us to study, from one side, the detail of rock and ledge on the overhang. The entire descent from lip to talus was about 200 feet. That was roughly two climbing rope lengths and required a landing shelf about halfway down in order to change ropes. From our previous reconnaissance we had spotted a suitable ledge for the change over. It was at least wide enough to support a pad of turf, grasses, and blooming flowers. It looked for all the world like a gigantic window box. ("What species of flowers would grow in a place like that?" "Shut up, Bradley, and start thinking rappel!")

We had two climbing ropes and decided to use them double so as to take them with us rather than leaving them hanging on the wall for later retrieval. That meant tying the two ropes together and looping the extended rope over a projecting rock at the top in such a way as to permit pulling the rope off from below after all had reached the ledge.

I led off to check the route before final descent. No problem. I ended up on the ledge and found several points for hanging the rope on second stage. The shelf was wider than we'd anticipated. It was almost like a sidewalk, but padded with grass and flowers. A bower. A gorgeously comfortable place to bivouac on a climb, wasted on a rappel. I signaled the others to come ahead. When they arrived they were ecstatic at the beautiful balcony and the vista of Unalaska from it.

After a decent time for enjoyment, we stood up and started preparation for the second stage. No sooner were we standing, when I felt a movement under foot and heard the growl of grinding rock. I yelled warning and with no more than that the entire ledge dropped out from underneath us. As the vegetative carpet peeled off the cliff in front of me, I saw a diagonal crack in the rock face and jammed both hands into the crack. The ledge was gone and between my dangling legs I saw it crash a hundred feet down on the talus with an explosion of rock fragments, soil, and flowers.

From my clinging point, I looked desperately around for my colleagues. They were all there! Each one had found something solid to grab. I couldn't believe it. We all should have been part of the rubble below, yet here we all were. In a few minutes we had regrouped on the shattered remnant of the giant window box and sat down to get our nerves back into order. The necessity of getting down off the face of the cliff helped cool the visceral uproar. I worked my way over to the rope, selected the marked end, and started to pull it off the invisible projection at the top. For about thirty feet there was no problem. Then the rope stuck. I changed position and got another twenty feet before it jammed again. Now, no matter what I did, it wouldn't come. I flipped, jerked, sent waves up the rope. No go.

New problem: if we couldn't get the rope down, there was no way to finish the descent other than suicide. To go up, there was no way even to start without trusting completely the jammed single strand. The last twenty feet of our descent to the ledge was unclimbable without going hand over hand up the rope.

How was it stuck? What was holding it? So that was the choice: the impossible or the treacherous. I had gotten us here, so it was my move. No drawing of straws. I told the gang that when (if) I got to the top I would cast off the rope. They could reset it and complete the rappel to the bottom. I would walk down as we had come up and meet them near the foot of the cliff. They should hang on to the rope no matter what. It would be their only way down.

I grabbed the rope and went up the first twenty feet, hand over hand, as though I trusted it, but expecting any moment to feel it let go above and send me to my ancestors. From there, without touching the rope I climbed up to the other loose end. The rest was a piece of cake. The rope had jammed in a V-shaped notch on the outcrop. The more I'd pulled, the tighter it got. Whew!

Perhaps the strangest aspect of this experience was that I was not defrocked for having placed the entire commissioned staff of the school in jeopardy. From the standpoint of education this was the first and most vivid lesson of many concerning the instability of mountain slopes in the Aleutian Islands. Volcanic rock often is highly fractured because the lava chills so rapidly after extrusion. On top of that, the wet climate, where the temperature swings back and forth over the freezing point almost daily, increases the effect of frost shatter. Finally, the tendency for plants to develop footing by driving their roots into the rock fissures further increases the instability while creating a treacherous green carpet. It really took us quite a while to decide that in spite of all the rock climbing skills and techniques we had learned in the 10th Mountain Division, the Aleutians demanded something else entirely.

The only permanent penalty I carry as a scar from that day on the cliff is a recurring dream where I wake up yelling and grabbing for a disappearing hand-hold. I lie there sweating and shaking, so loaded with adrenaline there can be no more sleep that night. I was just getting this story under way when the nightmare returned after forty-six years. It's just as good as it ever was.

FLASH! MTC VANISHES

The date was July 3, 1944. For about a month now our team of twelve, on detached service from the Mountain Training Center at Camp Hale, had been helping Major Forrest build the North Pacific Combat School. We had another month to go before our assignment ended and we would be returned to home base and the 10th Mountain Infantry Division. The NPCS already had a cadre of about thirty with more being added each day. They were rugged outdoor types and were becoming a competent instructional team. Things were moving ahead nicely—that is, until the mailman arrived.

That big packet of orders from Camp Hale that he dumped into Capt. Gordy Stimson's lap deserves the adjective "shocking." Shock one: The Mountain Training Center, "old MTC," our headquarters, and the hub of the special program that trained the 10th Mountain Infantry Division, no longer existed. Its mission had ended. Shock two: the whole Mountain Training Group including our detachment had been transferred to the

10th Infantry Division. What's this? No more 10th Mountain Infantry Division? Unlikely to be an error. Our twelve were thoroughly jolted and there were more shocks to come.

The orders were dated June 17. Presumably they had been en route almost two weeks. Along with them came an avalanche of personal communications from our buddies at Camp Hale. It was a grand mixture of information and rumor, good news and bad news, agony and ecstasy, helpful hints and gloomy resignation.

Under these circumstances one needs to be selective. I selected a letter from my buddy of Mt. Rainier days, Lt. Ralph Bromaghin. He was a wacky character but savvy, now a line officer. His observations: The 10th Mountain Infantry was packing up to leave for Texas. Its name would be changed to 10th Light Division or 10th Division and its personnel would be given "flat land" training with tanks, trucks, heavy artillery, and hot weather. No question that they were getting set for a combat mission.

From Captain Woodward, C.O. for the defunct MTC, came a hint that the problem of absorbing into the combat units the more than thirty commissioned officers and the more than one hundred noncommissioned officers of MTG was creating an uproar of dislocation. It was too much rank to be swallowed in one gulp. If any of our detachment wished to stay with NPCS it could probably be arranged. I read this as: if you come back you will cause us more trouble than if you stayed. Noncommissioned officers might lose rank and pay or be shipped out to other outfits since they had had only minimal combat training.

A letter from my brother Bill informed me that he had applied for officer's training before the ruckus started, and that unlike the earlier candidates he was not going to be allowed to return to the 10th after his commission.

Major Forrest indicated he would be happy to take on any of our detachment who wanted to stay. I asked about requesting Bill but he said that would not be possible.

It was time for another head-knocking session with our detachment, now feeling more detached than ever. Most of us had been with the 10th since it started on Mt. Rainier as Company A of the 87th Infantry Regiment. Loyalty ran very high among these charter members. They were also aware of a certain amount of jealousy arising from their being considered among the elite of the mountaineers who got those wonderful detached assignments, like our two months in the Aleutians. All wanted to return to the 10th but were more than a little let down by the idea that they might well lose rank, pay or be shipped out to other outfits. We had a couple of weeks yet to think it over, since our tour of duty with NPCS ran until the first of August. So Gordy and I urged the gang to take the time. Besides, there was a thought beginning to take shape in my head that I wanted to discuss with Gordy before I made my own commitment.

When we were alone I tried to give it words. "There are two things we should think about. They are related. The first is that now MTC is gone, the only mountain military training agency anywhere in America is right here in NPCS. The war is not yet over and there are lots of mountains between us and victory, both in Europe and Japan. There is only one U.S. division that is mountain trained. That's the 10th. It took a couple of years to get it into shape. What happens if the war goes on for a couple of years and attrition seriously reduces the strength of that one division? Where are the replacements going to come from? The 10th skimmed off most of the best civilian mountaineers in the United States. They needed only military training to be mountain soldiers. The next batch will take much more training. Do we, as part of the remnant trainers, have any obligation to consider this even though we have been given no authority to consider it? We apparently can stay with NPCS if we wish. Should we? Shouldn't we?

"The second point is a wild guess. Here we are in the frantic process of trying to train a team to get a task force dressed to enter the Kurils. The 10th is clearly getting ready for a combat mission. Is there a connection? Is the 10th going to be a part of that task force? How ready are they for Aleutian combat? Like us, hardly at all. There is lots we can learn in the next couple of months that could help them a great deal. They know us and trust us. I have this desperate feeling that we should stay right here and work at this job for all we are worth, so that we can be worth something. Remember that Major Forrest assumes NPCS will be a part of the firefight when that time comes. There's a good chance then that by staying here we'll be right with our buddies. What d'ya think?"

Gordy, always quiet and thoughtful, looked at me, at the wall, out the window, and finally back to me. "Worth thinking about. Let's let it simmer for a couple of days and then come back to it."

When Gordy and I got back together again he had made up his mind to return to the 10th, and I had made up mine to stay with NPCS. Gordy had no objection to my giving the noncoms my thoughts. In the end, T4g Fritz Ehrl joined Capt. Gordon Stimson in the return to the 10th Division. The rest stayed with me. As it turned out my hunch about the 10th was, like many another of my hunches, wrong. In retrospect it seems likely that the name change, the flat land training, and apparent disbanding of the 10th may have been simply to throw enemy intelligence off the track. When they finally hit the beach at Anzio, Italy, it was as the 10th Mountain Division.

Mt. Makushin

It was time for the trip to the summit of Mt. Makushin, highest mountain on Unalaska (6,680 feet), a volcano active enough to make noises and have a good-sized vapor plume. It was also lofty enough to have its own private crown of ice, the only glacier on the island. All these royal qualities make Makushin king of Unalaska.

Our team was getting restless for something bigger than ridges and gorges. The MTG gang especially was getting itchy to leave the soggy tundra behind and start some survival and mobility education on ice. A fresh issue of ice axes lent class to the expedition, bringing the morale and sense of anticipation up to a new level. Our C.O. was all steamed up to show off the mountain he'd bested three years before. He also had a couple of surprise extras for the trip.

Major Forrest was the only one among us who had seen General Buckner's orders to include amphibious training on the agenda. In addition, unknown to the rest of us, he had acquired a Studebaker "Weasel," a small tracked vehicle, also known as M-29C. Being an inventive person and knowing his Aleutians, he had designed and had fabricated a portable bridge to help it across the smaller gorges. The bridge consisted of two reinforced wooden beams somewhat longer than the Weasel. They were carried lashed, one on each side of the vehicle. The idea was to lay them over a gulch at the correct track gauge and drive across. If the system worked, the Weasel could lug our supplies and gear over at least the first leg of the climb.

Five miles west by north across Unalaska Bay, the Makushin River carries melt water from the glacier off the east flank of the mountain and drains into the sea where its gravelly delta is redistributed by the waves into a broad curving beach. That beach was the site of our first amphibious landing and our jumping-off point for the climb. The numerous braided channels of the river were to be the testing ground for the bridge.

The landing craft, so called, turned out to be a barge—an ancient but honorable barge, towed by a small motor tug. It carried comfortably all the warriors and their gear plus the Weasel and its bridge. The day was beautiful and the winds calm.

It took about an hour to cross the bay. The tug then nudged the barge, stern first, onto the beach and withdrew to deeper water while the group disembarked. The tailgate dropped with a crash and splash and, with the help of all hands, the Weasel crept off and up the beach. The rest of us shouldered our packs and splashed ashore. It all seemed awfully unheroic, too much like a picnic. Well, there was no rule that we couldn't enjoy it. What a day and what a valley! It was perhaps two miles wide where we were, stepped with broad terraces, emerald green and decorated with large iris blooms.

The bridge test was short. There were places where it functioned okay but there were many more where, even with a lot of manpower and four-letter words, the stream topography proved too stubborn an opponent of man's machinery.

Makushin Valley, crossing stream

Amphibious landing en route to Mt. Makushin

Major Forrest, after a fair test within a few hundred yards of the beach, called it quits and told the driver to return to the barge—er—amphibious landing craft, and take the Weasel back to Dutch Harbor. Our hopes that the Weasel would carry our packs at least to the head of the floodplain went down the drain. We shouldered them and slogged up the valley, wading the streams where necessary. Those of us from the 10th Mountain Division had already had some experience with the Weasel. I think most of us were relieved to go back to legs and rucksack instead of counting on a vehicle that had failed us so many times and in so many ways, especially in the mountains. There was another thing, harder to express. The noise and smell of an automotive vehicle clanking and crunching through a flowering alpine valley was hard on the spirit. I, for one, was cheered as the growl and scent of the gasoline engine faded away and was replaced by the scent of flowers and the integrated rhythm of lung and limb.

The day was warm and the backpacks heavy. In a short while individual clothing adjustment began to take place. I mention this because my pre-10th Mountain infantry experience on the flat lands of Illinois and Ft. Benning, Georgia, taught me that, while on duty, individual adjustments to anything were out. Adjustment was by order of the commanding officer. But individual adjustment of clothing was a thorny topic that came to a head very early in the history of the 10th Mountain Infantry Division. On the one hand were the mountaineers, most of whom knew little about running an army. On the other hand were the colonels and generals, most of whom knew little about coping with mountains. In this debate the mountaineers were able to sell their point: viz., if we must have frontline soldiers, it is best to have them healthy.

Metabolism varies considerably among individuals, and in the mountains men tend to be healthier if they keep perspiration at a minimum. Though days may be quite warm, nights can be very cold. Wet clothes out of doors can raise health havoc when the severe evening chill sets in. The problem is exacerbated by Aleutian weather where fog, rain and wind on the outside conspire with perspiration on the inside to wet a guy down, no matter what he does. For test purposes, our solution was, "adjust your clothing so that you are always a little chilly." That not only kept perspiration down but gradually toughened us all physiologically to the colder weather ahead. Later, as the savage wet-cold storms came on, we refined this advice to include clothing adjustment underneath the wet weather gear.

So picture us at this time, with one man wearing hat, sweater and jacket, another who has stripped to the waist, still another wearing a shirt with sleeves rolled up. No two men looked the least uniform. And that was the uniform of the day. I couldn't help smiling and thinking, "General Buckner, wherever you are, take it easy. All is well."

We made camp a little earlier than planned. We had been trudging up Makushin Valley. Behind us about eight miles, at the end of the trough, we could still see our landing site. The sky was clouding over. A rain storm was imminent. It seemed like a good moment to pitch tents and get under cover for the night.

Gordy Stimson and I had often camped in the shelter of a mountain tent and its navel. In jig time the stove was out, pumped up, and burning. The tent was instantly warm. We opened the two vents at the apex of the tent to prevent carbon monoxide accumulation, took off our outer clothes, had supper and bedded down to the drumming of rain and the slatting of

Makushin Valley, bivouac

Makushin Bay landing site.
Return march, Unalaska

wind. We had a minuscule haven in a world of storm. It was good to be camping again.

We woke to a wet and foggy world, but the rain had quit. By the time we finished breakfast the fog was lifting. The summit of Mt. Makushin was still five or six miles away and 5,000 feet above us up in the clouds. Major Forrest indicated that we could, without undue effort, reach the top and get back to camp before nightfall. So we left the tents in place and took only the gear we would need for the climb.

As we continued up Makushin Valley it began to narrow and steepen considerably. What had been a river flowing silently on a flood plain was now a brawling creek, tumbling over boulders and ledges. The green lush cover of the lower valley thinned, and became patchy with volcanic rubble showing between the patches. Finally we were walking over rock, rubble, and an occasional snowfield. Up ahead we could see the lower skirt of the glacier that caps the summit. To the east under the cloud deck the air was clear and we could see over fifty miles, past the small island of Akutan to Unimak, the first island off the Alaskan peninsula, its three volcanoes, like Makushin's summit, hidden in the clouds. It is one thing to read about a mountain range partially drowned in the sea and another thing to see it and feel it.

The terrain and footing were beginning to demand close attention. Makushin Valley finally heads up into innumerable small steep gullies cut by the glacial melt waters. Some of the material was poorly cemented, well-rounded gravel that was easily dislodged and went bounding down the chutes to the concern of those below. Another material was shattered lava in a clay matrix. It made a fairly solid mass but the moisture that was present produced slippery footing. A minor fall on this rasp-like material carried a higher than normal penalty on clothing and skin. A few of us had bleeding palms to remind us not to stumble.

A group of our enlisted men had already reached the top of the headwall. Some were cutting willow wands to mark our trail on the glacier, in the likely event that our descent would be made in a fog. It is an easy thing to find the top of a cone in a fog. Just keep climbing. There is only one top. The descent is another matter. The choices are infinite and a slight error on the line of descent can mean many miles off target at the bottom. Willow wands are a very comforting sight in a whiteout.

Capt. Gordy Stimson, Lt. Harry Hitchcock and I were "file closers," making sure no one was left behind. Our party was getting fairly well strung out. We were ascending a spur of the sharp-toothed material, watching our footing carefully, and were several hundred feet below the lip of the headwall. From that position we could not see the group above very well when the uproar broke out. Someone (Tapley?) shouted, "There goes Quick!" Whatever was going on didn't sound good. We put on the pressure but the going was tricky enough so that it was some time before we joined them. I recall arriving just as Har Quick struggled up to the top of a narrow chute. A rope around his waist held by friends at the top prevented him from falling back. A buddy by his side, also supported by a rope, carried Har's knapsack and steadied him on the climb. Har was using his ice axe as a cane, leaning on it heavily with each step of his right leg. He was smiling wryly at the cheers, but his face looked a bit gray. From head to toe the front of his clothes was shredded down to the skin and he was bleeding from innumerable scrapes and scratches. Obviously he had had a bad ride down the sharp-toothed chute. "For God's sake, man," I asked, "Why didn't you wait for more help?" "Aw," he said, "I didn't want any of these young kids to see weakness at a time like this." We eased him down on a pile of duffel to debate our next move.

Har's account of the fall follows:

> I was proceeding along the rim (of the headwall) and looking down at the roaring, turbulent river below. This is one of the few clear memories I have of the occasion. Suddenly I realized that I had taken a step forward onto a residual patch of black ice, camouflaged in a covering of volcanic dust. The slope of the ice was not particularly steep, probably no more than four or five degrees, but my feet slipped and I was on my way. Below the ice the slope was very steep, much too steep to stop. It ended in a vertical cliff, twelve to fifteen feet high, followed by another very steep pitch that ended in the cataract. I recognized the danger of rolling into the river but for some reason felt confident of surviving.
>
> Before I was off the ice I had rolled over into an 'ice axe arrest' position [stomach down, sliding feet first, body on top of ice axe handle, one hand on the handle, the other around the head, forcing the pick down into the ground to act as a brake]. After some seconds of a fast, rough ride on my stomach, I pitched over the vertical wall, lost contact with the ground, rolled in midair and landed hard on my right hip. Still holding my ice axe, I flipped over again into the ice axe arrest position. After some unknown distance I finally came to a stop just above the cataract.
>
> At this time all I can remember is the sense that I must not move for fear of dislodging the ice axe and

> plunging into the river. So I simply froze and waited for help. Someone, I don't know who, rappelled down to me, I don't know how.

Har had fallen almost 300 feet, more than double the length of a climbing rope (120 feet) and knots make rappelling difficult. It was an amazing demonstration of cool-headedness, training, and determination to survive in the face of a terrible pounding and abrasion. It was also comforting to note the speed and skill of the rescue. Obviously the team was in good shape.

Quite clearly Har was in no condition to continue the climb. We organized an evacuation team of two to help him back to camp while the rest continued the climb to alert the major with the advance party, who were now specks on the glacier. Har had been so successful in his refusal to show weakness that no one, not even Har, knew the extent of the damage. His real suffering now commenced as the many injuries he had sustained began to make themselves felt. How Har made the long hike back to camp with a fractured pelvis, I'll never know. Before his buddies got him into his sleeping bag he was in shock, and they all knew that the damage was more serious than any of us had suspected.

The rest of us resumed the climb. The major and his gang were now lost in the clouds but they had left their tracks in the snow and ice. The cloud deck continued to rise and visibility was good by the time we reached the rim of the crater, where the parties reunited. Major Forrest listened carefully to the account of Har's fall and the arrangements for evacuation. He nodded and suggested a hasty look around the summit and an early departure.

So we put our attention on the crater. It begged for attention. From the center of that ice-filled bowl there emanated a steady deep-throated roar that rattled the eardrums and shook the ground. But there was nothing to see except a round blue hole in the ice about 100 feet across. The uproar was coming from the hole but nothing else was visible. What was going on down there?

We closed in around the hole but not too close. The sense of a tremendous unseen power on the loose was intimidating. We could feel the increasing warmth as we approached. Out of curiosity I lobbed a fist-sized chunk of lava into the hole—at least that was my intent. As it arched over the opening it suddenly took flight and sailed up into the sky.

Had we examined the sky first we might have noted the transition zone where the superheated steam column condensed and became the long vapor plume, the hallmark of King Makushin. The ice in the crater slopes gently toward the blue hole, indicating its slow creep into the abyss. At that close range, we were pushed to grapple with the idea of a heat source so intense and extensive as to convert the whole annual snow accumulation of the crater into a column of steam thundering to the sky year after year.

On the rim of the crater the ice cover thins and exposes raw lava bedrock. Here we found fissures where escaping vapor was at a nonthreatening scale, and chilly mountaineers could warm up. One of my treasured slides shows George Gagnon, ice axe in hand, climbing rope over his shoulder, sharing a steamy warm spot with Ernest Tapley, Captain Krause, and a couple of other colleagues. The rocks around them are coated with crystals of pure yellow sulphur deposited from the vapors. In spite of the

Summit of Makushin, on rim of crater

Makushin crater rim, Unalaska

volcanically polluted air they were breathing, they all look relaxed and happy but distinctly unmilitary.

We left the summit of Makushin hastily in concern for our injured colleague back at camp. But my first close look at a live volcano is one of my most vivid memories.

The next morning the major and a portion of our party broke camp at the head of Makushin Valley and headed directly for the bay with Har, who could only move very slowly even with help. That painful trip took two days. The rest of us went overland to get help. After twenty-five miles, three mountain ranges and two days, we reached Dutch Harbor. We rounded up a doctor, got the use of the landing craft again, crossed the bay and picked up the rest of the crew.

Har was found to have a fractured pelvis. Since Unalaska had no facilities to treat him, he was shipped to Seattle. By this time it was apparently too late to pin his pelvis together so he was put in a cast to heal as best he could without pins and then was discharged. After the war Har joined the University of Colorado Geography Department where, at about the same time, my brother Bill was chairman of the geology department. In spite of their lower limb impairments, they ski together again as in the days of MTC. As far as I know, however, they have given up their special brand of Mumblety-Peg.

BEETS AND THE INSTANT EPIDEMIC

I almost hesitate to write up this episode—but not quite. Early post-war discussions with old buddies yielded several different versions, including one nonversion. So it seems the gates are wide open for the truth—my version.

Picture Unalaska in late July. NPCS has been in existence for a month and the team is shaping up well. The men are enjoying each other. We are all learning quite a bit about the Aleutians. Like any good army unit we tend to move on our stomach. Army meals are a mixed bag, and the second most favored topic of discussion—sometimes quite heated. The daily output of energy that goes with mountain trooping gave our guys wonderful appetites. They usually sailed through their meals with nary a backward glance. So it was something of a surprise at first to hear a tad of muttering about how often we seemed to be eating beets. Come to think of it, beets were now showing up at lunch as well as dinner.

Conversation with the mess sergeant revealed that he, too, was getting sensitive about the beets, but the truth was that we, along with the rest of Unalaska, were fast running out of all produce except beets. Dutch Harbor was a small military base, rapidly becoming part of the backwash in a fast moving war. The mess sergeant pictured the T-bones and ice cream going to the South Pacific while the North Pacific got the beets.

Evidence was on his side when we finally started to see beets at breakfast. The mess sergeant did his level best. He did things with beets no one had ever done before—or since: boiled, fried, creamed, pickled, soup, pancakes, au lait, au jus, au parmesan, au etc. If we didn't have beet ice cream it was only because the mess sergeant didn't think of it.

Everyone will remember the day when a ship pulled into the harbor. Our men were drooling when the order came to turn in our excess rations and draw new rations. Cheers went up from NPCS and we went about our duties with renewed vigor. The mountaineers went up into the mountains and made like young goats—except for Sergeant Niss, who had a sprained ankle. Our truck driver and Jake, his assistant, put two big sacks of beets into the truck and took off for the commissary.

It was 2:25 P.M. Bob Niss was bathing his ankle in a pan of warm water. Suddenly a wave of acute dizziness hit him. He crawled to his bunk and his last thought before he passed out was, "Those damn beets!"

Up on the mountain one of the squads under the leadership of Toni Matt had finished a difficult stretch of rock climbing and were resting on the tundra while Toni critiqued the climb. A sudden wave of nausea hit him. He sat down quickly and tossed up his share of the last beet ration, swearing quietly in Austrian.

On the road to town with those last sacks of beets our truck driver braked to a halt and said, "Jake, take the wheel, will you? My eyesight is really doing screwy things. I betcha it's those beets." He got out and started to walk around the truck. Before he reached the cab, two huge rock falls peeled off the high steep road cut and crashed down on the road, one just in front of the truck and one behind. The truck was completely blocked but untouched. The driver's eyes had snapped back to normal. Up on the mountain, Toni Matt, still sitting on the ground, was feeling much better, almost enjoying the quivering and bouncing of the tundra under him. Back at the barracks, Sgt. Bob Niss opened one eye and watched the water in the basin rocking and slopping onto the floor.

We had just received a special message from the Aleutian gods. "When experiencing an earthquake, don't believe all you feel. The chances are beets had nothing to do with it."

On the average we felt earthquakes every two or three weeks while we were in the Aleutians. It's a busy place, geologically speaking. The earthquakes seemed to be of two types: a silent rocking or rolling as in this case, or one with a directional three-stage sequence that made you wonder what had just run over you. First there was a distant rumble getting louder as it rushed at you, then a sharp jolt from below that rattled your teeth, and finally the rumble diminishing in the distance. The whole experience probably lasted less than ten seconds. These days the interpretation would be that at least some of the quakes are the result of the Pacific crustal plate suddenly slipping a little further under the North American crustal plate.

After the bulldozers cleared the road, our truck driver continued on to the commissary, turned in the two sacks of beets, drove around to the other side and took on the new rations. Yup—two sacks of beets.

Oddly enough there is a happy ending to this story, no thanks to the military. The Aleutian gods turned out to be on our side after all. Forget the beets. This was the day when some of the Unalaska streams were invaded by the leading elements of the 1944 salmon run.

BALLYHOO, FAREWELL, AND AN AIR CIRCUS

The last couple of weeks of July and the first week of August seem now to be a chaotic mix of brief episodes. Knowing Major Forrest, I'm sure organization continued to underlie most of our activities. Even the major was not above combining recreation with training. For instance, there was an annual foot race to the top of Mt. Ballyhoo. It was open to all comers. One of the comers was a navy man who had run and won the race for the last several years. This time he had come to Dutch Harbor from Seattle just for this race. It took place on Sunday—a day well known for rest and relaxation. No one was required to run, but the major strongly urged us, if you know what I mean. There was nothing tricky about it. It was a fairly steep slope with the usual lumpy coarse vegetation but nothing treacherous. The vertical climb was about 1,500 feet. In spite of the urging, a few of our gang didn't run. The fact that I remember no details of the climb itself suggest a questionable blot on my record. But at least the final results are clear. This was the year when the navy man took second place. Major Forrest was third. To no one's surprise, at least in NPCS, first place by a comfortable margin went to T. Sgt. Ernest "Tap" Tapley with the steel legs.

Part of my feeling of chaos for those three weeks has to do with current retrospective overlays on my memories. At that time we did not know that we were living our last days on Unalaska. A major shift in our affairs and geography was about to take place. Part of the feeling comes, I am sure, from the split up of our MTC gang. Some time in that period Capt. Gordon Stimson and Fritz Ehrl packed up to leave for Texas to rejoin the 10th (non-Mountain?) Division. It was a wrenching time for the gang. We had worked hard together for two years. Clearly some sort of military action was pending. Would the 10th show up in the Aleutians en route to the Kurils? I hoped so but perhaps I had doubts, because I recall asking Gordy to keep in touch. We needed feedback from the front line to evaluate the effectiveness of our training program. Gordy was also carrying an invisible request from me. "When you get back to the states, please call Maynie and tell her I won't be home for a while."

We all went out to Dutch Harbor to see them off. After they had gone, Harry Hitchcock and I decided to prowl around Mt. Ballyhoo a bit. At the southwest end of that big whaleback is the most incredible aircraft runway you can imagine. It was carved out of the steep slope almost like a kitchen shelf and was none too wide or long. When I think of the fog, the savage winds, the local turbulence a mountain like Ballyhoo could generate, and the state of the art in landing assistance of that day, my gizzard gets tight just contemplating the problem. In due time I would learn firsthand the courage and skill of the Aleutian pilots.

There at the airport I met my first antiaircraft telescope. To operate it you sat on a seat that was adjustable in height to bring your eye on line with the scope. Then with two hand cranks you adjusted the scope for direction and elevation. When you were seated, you and the chair moved as an integral part of the scope. The mechanism and optics were flawless. It was the most marvelous gadget I'd ever played with. While I was scanning around getting used to the cranks, I spotted a whale surfacing and spouting a couple of miles away. Then I tipped the system back to look at some of the mountains. Suddenly I was lost. Into my field of vision there appeared two soaring ravens seemingly so close that I could have counted their tail feathers. What they were doing, however, was so fascinating I skipped the tail feathers and concentrated my new cranking skill on following along with them.

The ravens were engaged in aerobatics, some of which would have tested any stunt pilot. For instance, one raven in straight and level flight was carrying some prize in its beak. Behind and higher, a second raven went into a power dive, leveled out at high speed behind the first raven, did a half roll as he sped by underneath and nipped the prize right out of the mouth of number one. Still at high speed, he completed the roll casually and was gone.

I must have spent at least an hour glued to the scope, watching these amazing creatures. The most common maneuver might be called a half roll and return. It was executed spontaneously for no discernible reason and often in a rhythmic series, spaced about eight to ten seconds apart, each half roll and return punctuated by a single "HAW!" on completion. Twice I saw a raven execute a true loop. The first was well done. On the second try he pulled out so fast that he appeared to stall and go into a spin. He fell as though he had been shot, flopping around wildly out of control. For 2,000 feet he fell this way, and I was holding my breath as he hurtled toward the sea. Just before he hit, his wings came out and he sailed away just above the water. In fact, the ravens seemed to enjoy this out-of-control fall. I saw it several times. On one occasion, two soaring ravens got into a quarrel over some goody. Paying no attention to flight or altitude, they wrestled and tumbled out of the sky for at least a thousand feet. They separated and pulled out just before crashing.

The time was July. Perhaps this behavior had to do with courtship, but a lot of it looked more like horseplay to me. Harry Hitchcock had been watching with field glasses while I hogged the scope. By the time we left, both of us were completely hooked on *Corvus corax* and kept our eyes searching for them from then on. In fact the whole training group became addicted, and mealtime conversation often started with, "Guess what those black clowns did today!"

Portfolio

1. *Russian church, Unalaska*
2. *Troops on Mt. Newhall; Mt. Makushin, background, Unalaska*
3. *Russian cemetary, Unalaska*
4. *Toni Matt and assistant, sketch mapping, Unalaska*
5. *Harry Hitchcock crossing river, Unalaska*
6. *Climbing Mt. Makushin. Akutan and Umiak Island in background, Unalaska*
7. *Clamming, Shagak Bay; Mt. Moffet, background, Adak*
8. *Adak airport*
9. *Shagak Camp looking south (view from outhouse), Adak*
10. *Typhoon, officers quarters; Kuluk Bay, background, Adak*
11. *Patrol on Mt. Moffet; Great Sitkin, background, Adak*
12. *Cape Yakak landing; Bay of Waterfalls, background, Adak*
13. *Mt. Moffet from Shagak Bay, Adak*
14. *Adak airport in late evening*

1

2

3

Toni Matt
Sketch Mapping

4

HARRY HITCHCOCK
Aleutian September Morn - July 15 1944
DUTCH HARBOR

5

6

7

9

10

11

13

14

Part II

Changing Directions

Preceding page: Squall over Thunder Bay, Adak

New Beginnings

Some time in early August 1944 we received the welcome news that the censorship on our location had been lifted. Letters to the states flew high that day. I pictured the folks at home rushing to their dusty atlases for a quick lesson in geography. (Maynie already had me pinpointed). Prior to the war my only sense of what the Aleutians might be like came from Rudyard Kipling's *The White Seal.* After our arrival in Unalaska I stumbled onto a dog-eared volume entitled *Son of the Smoky Seas* by Simeon Oliver, an autobiography by an Eskimo who had been raised in the orphanage at Unalaska and later went on to become a concert pianist, playing for audiences in the United States. I also found *Journey into the Fog,* the story of Bering's voyages, by Cornelia Evans. I enjoyed both these books and passed the titles on to Maynie and the folks.

At about this time Major Forrest disappeared for a few days on a mysterious assignment. Immediately after his return we received, with no warning, orders (SECRET again!) that the North Pacific Combat School (NPCS) was to move, lock, stock and barrel, to the island of Adak, 600 miles farther out the chain—600 miles closer to the enemy. The pulse stepped up its cadence a bit. Adak had been the secret base for the final drive to push the Japanese off Attu and Kiska. Two years before our move, Adak was an island devoid of people. With the help of the Alaskan Scouts and a gang of Seabees, Adak was converted in three weeks to the major American naval base in the Aleutians. In a few months more, with Adak as spring board, the Battle of Attu was underway.

Our move took place in three phases. The first was a real stunner. Our total allotted strength of six officers and seventy enlisted men was reduced to four officers and twenty-one enlisted men. More than two-thirds of NPCS was chopped off, dismissed, and disappeared. My first thought was "What in Hell?" My second thought: "Has there been a drastic change in mission?" If the mission remained the same, the change certainly made the assignment a lot tougher. We waited. No explanation was forthcoming—then or ever.

The second phase was an advance party led by Major Forrest to set up the arrangements in Adak for the main body. They would arrive later in phase three under the leadership of Captain Krause. I was assigned to the advance party with Lieutenant Hitchcock and three enlisted men, Bob Niss, our master sergeant, Lloyd Ahvakana, and Wilbern Lassing.

On the 10th of August, the advance party lifted off that groove in the nose of Mt. Ballyhoo called a runway. I could see the raw cut and outcrops rushing by just outside the small port facing my seat. Then we were out over the bay, ducking in and out of fog streamers as we banked slowly around until we were headed southwest, climbing toward our cruising altitude.

We were in the most trustworthy plane of the day, maybe of all time, a DC3. The accommodations were not exactly plush. Seats consisted of a shelf of aluminum bucket seats attached to the wall of the fuselage. Space was at a premium because about two-thirds of the fuselage was loaded with our gear and other freight piled to the ceiling and lashed down with rope and straps.

Adak, future airport and town.
Official photograph, U.S. Army Air Forces

There was one stowaway passenger not on the manifest. Major Forrest had acquired a half-grown Alaskan husky, a beautiful dog and well behaved. There being no more seats, he roamed the floor freely and made friends with everyone.

Our cruising altitude was probably around 12,000 feet, high enough to miss the volcanoes yet low enough to see some of them projecting through the cloud deck. The cabin was unpressurized but I don't recall anyone using oxygen. A few volcanoes, including our friend Makushin, were smoking. Occasionally we could look down through a hole and see a green island with a white collar of surf surrounded by the blue Bering Sea.

MOLENAAR LANDFORM MAPS
SEA
BERING
MT MOFFET
Shagak Bay
R
Shagak Camp
Bay of
Island
Bitchin Ridge
2
Bay of
Waterfalls
Cape Yakak

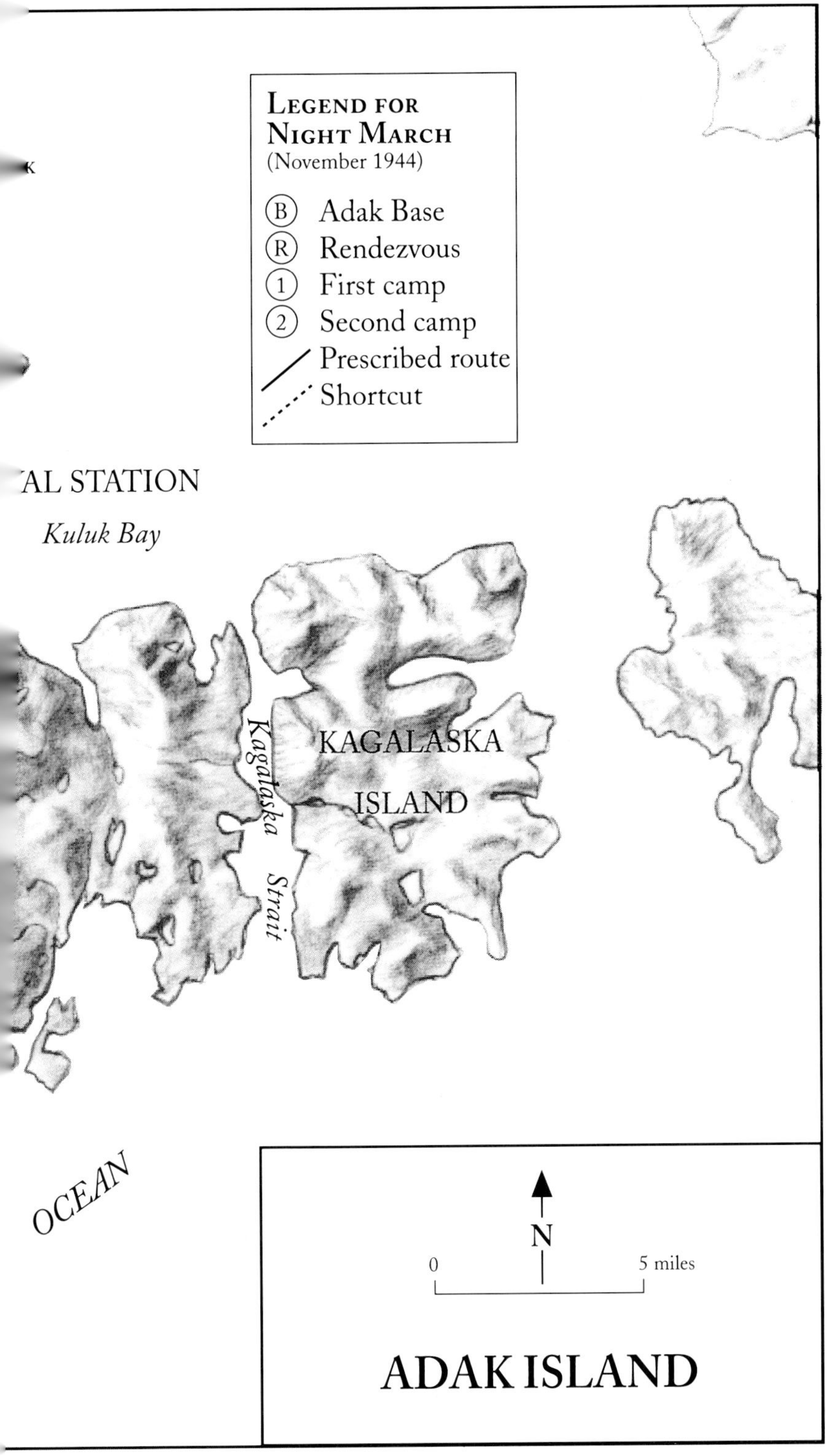
LEGEND FOR
NIGHT MARCH
(November 1944)
B Adak Base
R Rendezvous
1 First camp
2 Second camp
Prescribed route
Shortcut
AL STATION
Kuluk Bay
Kagalaska Strait
KAGALASKA
ISLAND
OCEAN
N
0
5 miles
ADAK ISLAND

We had one sad and mysterious casualty on that flight. The major's husky suddenly went into violent convulsions and died. The only clue was not entirely convincing. One of our gang had opened a can of meat for a snack and gave a small chunk to the husky who, doglike, gulped it down. Within a few minutes he was clearly in agony. Within the hour he was dead. Perhaps, as we gained altitude, the drop in atmospheric pressure produced sudden expansion of stomach gasses in the dog. In any case the young man who shared the snack remained unaffected.

The rules on board the DC3 were more flexible than those of today. There was no cabin door, and I was free to watch the pilot and copilot in action. In fact they invited me in as long as I did not get underfoot. They were a cheerful pair, chatting about the islands, the plane, navigation, the weather, and the lack of girls. It was an educational grab bag. Before we started our descent toward invisible Adak they became serious and intent, checking estimated position, clock, chart and other instruments, conferring over the radio with people on the ground. Looking at the big soft clouds rising to meet us I could not help wondering how many of them had volcanic cores. These were the days when radar was only a precocious infant. What was invisible to me was also invisible to the pilots.

The sunlight and sky were suddenly snuffed out. We were in a dark gray void unable to see as far as the wing tips. I watched the altimeter slowly unwinding and the compass slowly rotating while my viscera slowly tightened up like a guitar string. I knew from the instruments we were spiraling down but could feel nothing. It was eerie. Rain and snow were spattering the windshield and turning to ice. The wipers were unable to keep it clear. The copilot said plaintively, "You know, they never have worked. I think we oughta get them changed one of these days."

Bad landing on Mt. Adagdak

The pilot grunted and then glanced at me. Reading me perfectly, he grinned broadly, pointed to the instruments and said, "This is the time when you have to believe them."

Were the wings icing up? I could not see. The outside temperature must have warmed up a little. Proximity to the sea? In any case the ice on the windshield broke up into flakes that slid off into the slipstream. The rain, too, was streaming off cleanly while the wipers flailed wildly, doing nothing. The copilot shut them off in disgust. Then we broke through the cloud base. We were skimming over a large lagoon. On our right was a small volcano. Farther on was a bigger one. Both had their tops in the clouds, two of those invisible solid cores. The small one, we discovered later, had the remains of an airplane plastered on its flank.

Dead ahead now was our landing strip, generously wide and long. The far end, however, terminated abruptly against some rocky cliffs. Everything looked very gray and wet. Our landing created a wake like that of a sea plane. Long before we reached the rocky cliffs we were taxing toward a hangar. The pilot looked at me again and laughed uproariously. "Fun, eh?"

I was glad I had had the trip. I was glad the cloud deck was no lower. I was glad I was not an air pilot in the Aleutian Islands, and I was glad to be a mountain soldier with my boots on the ground.

Adak

When you've seen one Aleutian island you've seen them all. Well—sorta. Wet, cool, green, rugged, windy, treeless, yes. But Adak Island seemed quite a change from Unalaska, and Adak town and naval station were very different from Ft. Mears and Unalaska Village. Here was no backwash of World War II. Kuluk Bay was full of war ships slipping in and out. The airport was a busy place with both military and commercial traffic. People were moving around as though they had to get somewhere right away.

There was no Russian church and graveyard, no buildings with any look of history. In fact Adak town looked as though a typhoon-load of mixed Quonset huts and storage sheds had been blasted at the landscape and stuck where they hit. Many of the Quonsets were sitting in a deep trench hastily gouged out by a bulldozer. Some had cables stretched down across their roofs. As the weather moved forward toward winter, we appreciated these precautions against wind. Our Native colleagues told us that the original Aleut residences were mainly underground pits with a roof at ground level. There are times in the Aleutians when anything that sticks up above ground level is in jeopardy.

In one of the bulldozed trenches we saw a Quonset hut lying absolutely flat on the ground as though a Mark 4 tank had rolled over it. It had caved in during the previous winter under the snow load. We were beginning to pick up a few more items for inclusion in the curriculum on survival.

Adak landscape seemed fairly rugged but with considerably less relief than that of Unalaska. Rising immediately northwest of town was the highest mountain on Adak, Mt. Moffet. It was an extinct volcanic cone, carved up a bit by ancient glaciers and streams but with no present ice cap, nor any perennial snow fields. Its highest point (3,984 feet) is about half the altitude of Mt. Makushin on Unalaska. As I looked around, my immediate impression was that in terms of training mountain soldiers, we had lost rather than gained by the move to Adak. As time went on that impression deepened considerably.

Why had we changed? The easiest answer to that question was "Because we were ordered to." A more satisfying logic might be that Adak was the Advance Command Post for the Aleutians and the place where a task force would be staged for an attack on—well—Paramushiro, for instance. In spite of our trimming NPCS appeared to be still on target. Better call it "streamlined." The pressure was still on.

Our advance party reported to the base commander and in short order we were assigned quarters for the school and staff plus additional quarters for the trainees. In early September

Officers quarters on Palisades.
Kuluk Bay, background, Adak

Captain Krause and the rest of our team arrived. We were at full strength and ready to go—after certain chores.

For administration and mess facilities we were attached to the 768th Antiaircraft Artillery Gun Battalion. The school's location was on the northwest edge of town where, when the fog let up, we had an unobstructed view of Mt. Moffet. The NPCS officers' living quarters consisted of two snug Yakutat huts in a spectacular location about fifty feet from the edge of a 100-foot cliff looking south over Kuluk Bay. The location, called "the Palisades," was probably named by a homesick New Jersey soldier—well named. Like the original overlooking the Hudson River, this cliff face was basaltic lava standing in columns like a vertical stack of giant black hexagonal pencils, their bases at some unknown depth below the sea. By what good fortune were we assigned to such a superb setting? It was a place for generals and admirals. The question flicked through my mind and was quickly lost in the feverish preparations for our first class. Before the first class had graduated, I had my answer to that question.

Just now, with our first class scheduled for September 15, we had four weeks to learn what we could about the island and the naval base, gather together the mountaineering equipment and supplies for fifty candidates for two and a half months training, design, execute and publish from scratch a training manual with copies for the candidates, the teaching staff, and for the advance information and approval of the immediate military hierarchy. Four weeks looked awfully tight. My memory of that period seems more like an old film of the Keystone Cops than a well-planned military operation, but the fact that we ended up with most of the chores pretty well done suggests that a certain amount of order must have prevailed.

Probably our most important reconnaissance of the island was the first. The entire staff of twenty-five, under Major Forrest's leadership, climbed Mt. Moffet on the perfect day. It was the usual rotten rock, but with the route we took, it posed no threat. At the summit, with only a few small puffy clouds for decoration, we looked down on a magnificent relief map. Not only could we see the entire island of Adak but several of the neighboring islands both to the east and to the west. We got out our maps, notebooks, and binoculars and spent a couple of hours of study, with discussion about future small-group investigations of particular interest for the training programs. For instance:

Thirty miles east of Adak was Great Sitkin, a big active volcano capped by a glacier. Though inconvenient in terms of transporting, sheltering and feeding a large group of men, it did

Great Sitkin steambath in a fumerole

represent a possibility for glacier training if such was urgent. A few of us actually did reconnoiter Great Sitkin, but glaciers were finally dropped from the training program.

Three bays around the base of Mt. Moffet showed well-developed bay-mouth bars. These should be investigated for purposes of training in amphibious landings. (It was just as well we did investigate them before we tried a landing.)

There seemed to be no shortage of cliffs for training in climbing and rappelling, but most of them looked threatening from the standpoint of rotten rock. From this distance, the Palisades looked like one of the best possibilities. (Later it became the scene of a high-speed nightmare.)

And so on. For many days thereafter we would be following the leads that were uncovered that day on Mt. Moffet. I think there was some disappointment among at least the 10th Mountain men that all the really challenging summits were attached to neighboring islands, too far for a recreational ascent. We climbed Moffet many times before V-J Day but never again did we have such a vista.

Magnum Opus

Among the documents sent me by Colonel Forrest to help this story along is a faded, gray-blue, cloth-bound, three-ring, hard-back, loose-leaf notebook. The outside cover bears the title, "The Course of Instructions Given at the North Pacific Combat School," clearly hand-lettered around our escutcheon displaying crossed ice axe and rifle on a coil of climbing rope. May I be forgiven an extra heartbeat? Preparing that cover was my last act at the completion of our training manual.

For some reason, the binding rings have been torn out and the volume looks as though it had gone through the battle of Attu. But as far as I can determine, it is all there. The pages are in order—all 116 of them, plus Major Forrest's covering letter dated 5 September 1944 to the commanding general of the Alaskan Department, and the general's acceptance letter dated 14 September 1944. The general's comments (slightly streamlined) are quoted below.

1. This is an excellent and well prepared outline. Very interesting and basically sound.
2. We must not overlook the basic mission of the school. We are NOT trying to train expert infantrymen—but are trying to develop instructors who can take well trained infantrymen and top off their training with special instruction applicable to this climate and terrain. I want to emphasize this and insure that the commandant of NPCS keep this objective constantly in mind. Minimize the time spent in the school area—get them out in the field for progressively longer periods as the course develops.

In spite of a pace that continually threatened to override quality control, Major Forrest, Lieutenant Hitchcock, and Lieutenant Bradley had batted out that manual, profusely illustrated with sketches, maps and diagrams, in less then three weeks. The ink was only slightly damp when the first class of candidates arrived on September 15.

Among us all, there was little real combat experience. We were using our collective imaginations in the hope that what we knew of survival and mobility would somehow have practical consequences in the haywire of battle.

As I read over the manual, I am amazed at the sheer volume of material we threw into it, and am further amazed that the general of the Alaskan Department had so few critical comments. If he had known what we now know about the islands, he should have suggested that we prune the program to about half size. Or perhaps he knew that the pruning would happen anyway and be better without his suggestions. The field has a way of adjusting theory to reality. In the end, many of our instructional projects got lost in the time crunch or the priority crunch. On the other hand, certain projects we had overlooked suddenly landed in our laps with Top Priority written all over them. And, of course there were those events that cannot be put into any curriculum. They fall out of the sky once and we learn, whether we want to or not.

What follows contains a sampling of our educational experiences—and whatever else comes to mind, to illustrate our life on Adak. With our first fifty candidates things were bound to happen. At least we had our textbook.

The Mystery of Matsuwa

Shortly before the advent of our first class, Major Forrest approached me with, "Got a minute? Come on over to the house. I have some matters to consult with you on." "The house" meant his cabin on the edge of Palisades. We three junior officers occupied one of the two cabins; the major had the other. Very convenient for a conference. There was something in the major's voice that brought my insides to attention.

After some light discussion he plunged into the topic of the day. His voice was quiet but purposeful and he was watching me closely. "What we talk about today you mustn't mention to anyone, not even in your sleep." Without pausing to have me sign an oath, he pushed ahead. "It has to do with our combat mission. I have hinted at it before. When we finish training the

Preliminary Sketches for NPCS Field Manual

Rappel

Stages in the rappel

Front view of stirrup rescue showing arrangement of ropes and stirrups

3-man stirrup rescue

task force, NPCS will have completed its mission. We will then become the forward armed reconnaissance patrol, first ashore, the spearhead for the invasion. I will be in command of that patrol." He paused to let this new extension of our mission sink in. I was still breathing, so he added, "I will need an intelligence officer, an S-2. How would you feel about that assignment—starting now?"

How did I feel about it? Well, a bit numb perhaps. A lot of poorly organized questions can pour through a guy's brain at such a time. But this being the army, most of the questions were not to be asked out loud. How ready am I for combat? Not very. All my life I've leaned toward noncombatant solutions to my problems. I did manage to get through Ft. Benning with a bar on each shoulder. Before and since then, our Mountain Training Group was organized to teach survival and mobility in the mountains. Training in tactics was minimal but we knew that the firefight was up ahead. How ready is anyone for that first engagement?

What did I think of Major Forrest as a commanding officer and combat leader? He was young, intelligent, vigorous. I'd seen him, in field clothes and boots, throw a handspring right off the tundra. I'd never seen him take alcohol. From some remarks he had made I thought he was eager for battle. He was courageous. In fact, he seemed to have a bit of the daredevil in him, sometimes taking unnecessary risks. In combat, would he risk his men unnecessarily? Didn't know. I had the uneasy feeling that with his enthusiasm, we might all end up dead. Come to think of it, we were all going to end up dead anyway. Does it take an enthusiastic daredevil to lead a successful combat patrol? Maybe. Maybe so.

While all this uncomposted mental garbage was still flying by I had already said, "Don't know anything about the job of S-2 but I'll give it a go."

"Good," said the major. "Just continue with the mountain training assignment. The S-2 job will be an invisible sideline for the time being. Here are some manuals to study regarding S-2 duties. Come back when you have looked them over." "OK," said I. "I'm assuming that part of my assignment will be to find out all I can in advance about our target area. I've had considerable experience with maps and aerial photos. I'd sure like to get started on the target right away. You may recall that back at Dutch Harbor I introduced two or three of the MTC group to a method of sketch mapping applicable to military reconnaissance. If possible I'd like to introduce this into the curriculum for a few select candidates." The major gave me his best poker face and repeated, "Come back when you have studied the manuals."

So during the day it was working on the training manual and honing the team for the first wave of candidates. At night it was the S-2 manuals, voluminous notes, and diagrams. Those notes have not turned up in my Aleutian memorabilia and my memory of the manuals' content is now almost as blank as when I said, "I'll give it a go."

One jolting diversion occurred about this time. I record it here because of the unsettlement of mind and spirit it produced at a wrong time for me.

Our trucks, loaded with the training group returning from the field, were just coming to a stop when S. Sgt. George Gagnon vaulted over the tailgate. The truck behind was too close. George got pinned between the two. We rushed him to the hospital. In a short time we had the diagnosis: Pelvis shattered in six places, urethra ruptured. Another one of our most needed members out of action for the duration. In the morning I dropped in to see him at the hospital. He broke out his famous golden-toothed smile. "Don't know how I could have been so stupid," he said. "I'm awfully sorry. I apologize. I'll miss you guys." Next morning he was on his way back to the states.

How would the world get along without the George Gagnons? The guy who knows how to fix anything in the field. The guy who helps keep others out of trouble or helps them out if they get into trouble. The guy with the broad grin and quiet laugh that keeps spirits up. The small but powerful dynamo that drives the heartbeat of the outfit. How did we get along without George? Well, we did because we had to, but it was tougher going and not as much fun.

It took time to shake off the gloom of this second loss to the MTC team and the negative feelings I had about a combat reconnaissance assignment without George and Har.

When I handed the S-2 manuals back to Major Forrest about a week later, he handed me a roll of maps and an envelope of aerial photos. "The island of Matsuwa is our target. It lies about halfway down the Kuril chain from Paramushiro. The only maps we have were smuggled out of Japan a number of years ago, before the military base was constructed there. The aerial photos were taken by some of our planes operating out of Adak. They are pretty poor. The weather on Matsuwa is not any better than it is here. Fog, rain, heavy winds. And the distance is uncomfortably close to the fuel limit of the planes. A couple of pilots' lives are already part of the price of these photos. Make what you can of them."

Many weeks later I had to turn the maps and photos back, but I wish I could have kept just one map as a memento. Unlike our starkly businesslike USGS topographic maps, these were the handiwork of artists. The topographic lines were there of course, but in addition there were the delicate hand-wrought symbols of vegetative types (trees, yet!), exposed bedrock, boulders and sand, each expressed uniquely in color and design, making a knowledge of the written language almost unnecessary. It was easy for the mind to wander and to wonder about these people with whom we were locked in combat. Were these cartographers the same people who made the exquisite prints that hung in my parents' home, prints that I grew up with and loved?

Were these the same people who launched the treacherous attacks on Pearl Harbor and Dutch Harbor? The ones who conducted the death marches for their American prisoners, the ones who blew themselves up with hand grenades on the island of Attu and were now launching their suicidal kamikaze attacks on our fleet in the South Pacific? Oriental ethos was not my assignment, but . . .

Matsuwa is a small, roughly oval island, four by eight miles across, a single volcanic cone sticking up out of the sea. One of its last eruptions appears to have breached the southeast side of the crater, allowing a lava flow to pour through the gap and form a low pancake-like peninsula. That flat lateral extension of the cone is the only place that could be made habitable for humans. The rest of the cone is rough and steep, with its lower flanks chopped by the heavy surf into vertical cliffs. The presence of a few trees suggested winds less fierce than those of Adak.

The aerial photos showed the military base occupying the whole pancake. There appeared to be an anchorage and docks off the edge and a skimpy airstrip on top. The rest of the area contained a few buildings and an elaborate network of trenches and barbed wire. The Japanese looked ready for us.

It was difficult for me to visualize an armed combat patrol spearheading the attack with a surprise landing. If we parachuted onto the cone even in broad daylight, the chances were good that we would all have busted legs. If we tried to make an amphibious landing on the cliffs in that surf, the chances were good that we'd all be drowned. To land on the pancake would be a laughable non-surprise, and we'd all die of hyperventilation from too many bullet holes.

Start over. Could the Japanese on Matsuwa be bombarded and isolated from a distance until they surrendered? It was such a tiny base I couldn't believe it was important enough to warrant the attention of a major task force. A land-based army lieutenant does not expect to be in on the grand strategies of a naval show, but a land-based lieutenant is free to have a few bad nights as he contemplates what may be his role in that show. My main hope was that Matsuwa would prove to be such a stupid target that the strategists would think of something better to throw a skinny mountaineer at.

All these were thoughts I kept to myself. Meanwhile I set about creating overlays, transferring military information from the blurred photos to the map. Then, just to let the major know there were other potentially useful things I could do, I made some oblique sketches showing how the island would look from an airplane approaching from various directions and altitudes. I also made some silhouettes serving the same purpose for a man with his eyes glued to a submarine periscope. In spite of my worries about Matsuwa, there was a strange feeling of zest and relief in finally having a clear target.

"Looks good," said the major after glancing them over. I said, "If you can keep me supplied with air photos as they come in, I'll be able to give you a moving picture of developments on Matsuwa." "Right," said the major. He picked up the bundle and walked off. And that was it. I received no orders making me S-2. Matsuwa was never mentioned again. In a recent phone conversation with Frank Forrest, he remembered that "Paramushiro was always the target. Matsuwa? Where's Matsuwa?"

Bay-mouth Bars, a Blue Fox, and the Gastronomy of Survival

During the period when we were enslaved by the training manual, we would sometimes sneak off for a day of reconnaissance and renewal. From the summit of Mt. Moffet and on our maps of Adak, we had noted the bay-mouth bars across Andrew Lagoon to the north of town and Shagak Bay to the west. These represented potential sites for amphibious training. The bars are deposited by breaking waves carrying in and dumping material they have quarried from the headlands. I had seen many such bars across estuaries and embayments along the coast of Massachusetts. They are even a fairly common feature of inland lakes. That long curving cushion of sand on an otherwise rocky shoreline can be a comfort to a party in a small boat looking for a place to land.

The Bering Sea is not to be trifled with. Not only does it tend to be very rough but its temperature is such that in those pre-wetsuit days, a man overboard for more than fifteen or twenty minutes was considered to be beyond redemption. Thus a bay-mouth bar on the map of a rugged Aleutian coast looked like a benediction to us nonmarine types.

At first chance I took off on foot one morning, accompanied by one of our enlisted men, Bob, whose last name escapes me. He was a quiet, bright young fellow, active, well coordinated, and interested in anything new—good company for a reconnaissance. The bar across Andrew Bay on the north side of Adak was our target.

Long before we could see the coast, we could hear the thunder of the surf. By the time we were rounding the last spur in the lower east slope of Mt. Moffet, we could feel the ground vibrate from the shock of each breaking wave. Then before us was the beautiful curving two-mile-long bar across Andrew Lagoon. It was exactly as anticipated except that the sand grains making up this bar had diameters ranging from one foot to three feet. The incoming Bering surf was sweeping these boulders back and forth like ordinary sand grains but with a growling, bumping, grinding sound that harmonized well with the thunder of the falling combers. For me the sights and sounds conjured up visions of landing crafts exploding in splinters and legs being shattered as men attempted to wade ashore.

Bob and I sat on the spur immersed in thunder and thought for perhaps an hour, hypnotized by the magnitude and power of the scene. What Bob's thoughts were I don't know. Mine were censored. What would our landing on Matsuwa be like?

There is a low divide between the town of Adak and Shagak Bay that became the route for our second attempt to discover a

Andrew Bay and Bay Bar that isolates Andrew Lagoon

reasonably safe small boat landing site. Unlike the bar at Andrew Lagoon, the bar across the mouth of Shagak Bay has its center section under water, giving the surface appearance of two fingers pointing at each other from opposite sides of the bay. The heavy outer surf breaks on the bar as usual, but the smaller residual waves continue into the bay, carrying with them the finer material that makes up the inner beach. What Bob and I saw through our binoculars from the divide seemed like an excellent training site. The untrained candidates could learn the rudiments of making a landing in the comparative calm of the lagoon. Then they could graduate to the more difficult job of landing on the two fingers in much heavier surf. The only possible problem we could see was the product of small streams flowing into the inner bay, depositing material for a wide tidal flat and creating the risk of quicksand when the tide came in. Otherwise the whole setup looked far less lethal than the roaring boulder mill outside Andrew Lagoon.

"Hey! What's that?" Bob had his eyes glued to the binoculars which, in turn were glued to the tidal flat, now at low tide. "Something black running around down there diggin' holes." Sure enough, there was a little dark critter energetically sampling the tidal flat. It was too far for identification but he appeared to be about the size of a house cat or small dog—both unlikely this far from civilization. Land animals of any kind were rare in the islands. Instantly we reverted from educators looking for an outdoor classroom to primitive hominids stalking a little dark critter on a tidal flat. We moved rapidly from grassy hummock to grassy hummock down toward the bay, keeping at least one hummock between us and our prey, but stopping once in a while to sneak a peek at the critter. At one place we lost track of him, but while we were wondering what to do he came running out from behind his own hummock (a den?), heading for his private dig.

By now it was clear we were looking at a fox with a taste for sea food. But what species of fox? Its color, a dark slate gray, was like no other fox of my acquaintance. Later I remembered Har Quick mentioning a "blue fox" associated with the Aleutians. Still later I read about blue foxes making miserable Vitus Bering's dying days on the island west of the Aleutians that carries his name. So I presume we were stalking a blue fox. It turned out he (or she) was digging clams for the family who lived in a den dug into the tundra about eight feet above the tidal flat. Every time the clam bearer approached the den, three pups bounced out to greet him. They were ordered in again when he went back for another load. It finally dawned on us that the clam

Evening bivouac on survival march

bearer could bear only one clam at a time—a clam so huge that sometimes it could only be rolled with some effort across the soggy flat and up the bank to the den. Now, I like a shore dinner as well as anyone—even a fox. So I switched roles again and became a clam prospector. Abandoning my blind, I stood up and walked out on to the flat searching for clam siphon holes. The fox, seemingly unsurprised, sat down by his den and watched. In short order my grubbing fingers came up with the largest clam I'd ever seen.

In outline and shell thickness it reminded me of what we used to call "quahogs" on the east coast. The new improved name is "cherrystone clams." The largest quahog I'd ever seen on the east coast had a diameter of about three inches. This Aleutian relative spanned about ten inches. With a great deal of effort I finally worked my knife blade between the thick porcelain shells and opened my prize. It was a prize. The body inside on the half shell made me think of a squab on a platter. Here was clam on the half shell beyond my wildest dreams. Never mind the absent lemon. My well trained mouth opened automatically and—"Hey!" yelled Bob. He looked a little gray and his eyes bugged out. "What's up?" I asked, salivating like Pavlov's dogs. "Well, aren't cha going to cook him or assassinate him or anything first?"

It was too late. My whole visceral system was already locked into Clam Mode #1. In a few minutes the shell was clean. What a feast! But if anyone had told me in advance that I would ever consider one clam on the half shell a feast, I'd have laughed him out of town. This was the new era.

Bob was horrified but I won back his confidence a few weeks later when our first class went on its survival march during which, for three days, we had to subsist on whatever the island provided. On the first night out we camped near Shagak Bay and made a big bucket of clam chowder. Verily it was the Aleutian parable of the Loaves and Fishes. With only five clams, finely chopped, seasoned and boiled in their own juice, we fed the multitude and they pronounced it good.

Shagak Bay Chowder was justly famous and became a "must" for each class on its first survival march. But before the third class of fifty had gone, two shadows were falling. (1) Shagak Bay was running low on giant clams. Even the foxes had gone. (2) In all our prowling around Adak, we found no other source of giant clams. It was unsettling to learn that we had not been harvesting the clams, we had been mining them.

As our survival marches continued, we were gradually developing a gut feeling that the apparent opulence and vigor of life on these islands is a mirage. It is actually precariously poised, easily obliterated, slow to recover. In terms of human vision and attitude, how much of life on this planet is in the same fix today?

For those who may wish to learn more about the emergency foods we found useful on Adak, the following are some of the important protein sources:

mussels, etc.—Adak's tortuous rocky coast provides innumerable small coves, partially sheltered from the heavy open surf. In many of these we found mats of large blue-black mussels covering the rocks in the tidal zone. Steamed or in chowder, they made a fine meal. The coves and mussels were so ubiquitous we detected no evidence of over use. Our worst experience came in the mussels of Kuluk Bay. They werc so seasoned with diesel fuel from the marine traffic that for a week after a meal you would not dare burp near an open flame.

etc.—If you carried a net and had a generous allotment of time and luck you might capture a mess of shrimp or a couple of the big Aleutian crabs, magnificent eating but rarely enough to go very far.

waterfowl—During the migration season, waterfowl mobbed the beaches and shoal areas. Unfortunately for us we had no shotguns. A 30-caliber MI rifle and no retriever make for a wasteful massacre of these beautiful creatures. On one occasion two of our enlisted men watched a large hawk nail an emperor goose. The hawk was having a hard time boosting its trophy ashore and up to its perch. The men rushed the hawk, which saw them coming but could not get airborne. That night we had goose for supper and discussed the art of falconry. Just a thought.

salmon—During the salmon run we gorged on them. Ernest Tapley gave us a fast food demonstration. Lying down on the

Dead salmon in stream after the run

edge of the stream bank, he gently, slowly, put his hand down into the water. Salmon were streaming by his hand en route to the head waters. He caressed the belly of a passing fish that seemingly paused to enjoy the massage. Tapley's hand slid forward to the gills and he deftly tossed the salmon out on the bank.

For a period after the salmon run was over, potable water and breathable air became hard to find near any stream. They were clogged with dead and decaying fish. Thanks to the gulls, eagles, ravens, foxes and other scavengers, this period of nausea passed quickly. But so did the salmon as a source of emergency food. We'd have to wait for the next year's run.

ptarmigan—There were ptarmigan on Adak. They were not hard to find or to see and they tended to be slow moving on the ground. A good rifle shot who cared could drop one without damaging the edible portion, and they were delicious. However, these birds were not overly abundant. Our inroads on their population were apparent, and we urged the survival classes to use other foods if possible.

These were our main sources of food for the survival marches. It is quite obvious that our best bets for finding a meal lay along the coast, and of these, mussels were the surest. In season, salmon was a bonanza of gold. With a smokehouse we might have been able to stash away enough salmon to help get us through the winter. "Smokehouse" reminds me that the shore was not only our best supplier of food but the only supplier of the means to cook it—driftwood. We took great pleasure in knowing that our emergency fuel was a gift from our enemy, Japan, who sent it to us gratis and duty free in the arms of the Japanese current.

Trial by Rockfall, I

I am apt to jump around between military and civilian terms in remembering the NPCS educational program, so the following definitions may help:

NPCS	**Civilian Equivalent**
Commandant (Major Forrest)	Principal or Dept. Head
Instructor (Commissioned officers)	Teacher or professor
Guide (Noncommissioned)	Teacher or instructor
Candidate	Student or trainee

You would think that an event like the arrival of our first class of fifty candidates for mountain training would have remained as a memory in bas-relief. Yet all I can dredge up now is a wispy scene of the supply sergeant and me issuing mountain clothing and equipment to an endless line of faceless soldiers. What I do recall with vividness is our first overnight mountain excursion with that class. Picture, if you can—or dare, fifty greenhorns with heavy packs crawling up the steep treacherous east face of Mt. Moffet.

Of course we preceded the Moffet excursion with long hikes across the rolling tundra where the candidates had a chance to strengthen legs and shoulders and to check out their mountain gear as well as the new life style that went with it. We also introduced them to such details as the rappel and the slow measured pace of a mountain man going up hill. There was also the vertical body position for traversing steep slopes. Fear of falling sometimes causes a person to lean toward the wall which in turn may cause the footing to break out on the downhill side. "Stand in obedience to the law of gravity" is the rule. What we had not done yet was to put the candidates on any large steep slopes.

The instructional team itself had not yet tested the east face route on Moffet. We had seen it from below nearby and had no qualms about it for us. It was a typical product of the Aleutian climate and geology, a fairly steep slope of irregular giant steps with tundra treads and rocky risers transected by spurs and gullies. The main danger would come from the unseen rotten seams and joints in the rock beneath the green mantle. Sudden slope failure and rock fall were distinct possibilities, especially with untrained personnel. The slope angle was probably close to fifty degrees. That does not seem steep until you stand on it and realize that if you should stumble and fall you might easily get into a long, rough, and uncontrollable descent. The instructional team would probably not have bothered with a climbing rope which can limit a person's ability to dodge rocks. To a person untrained in the use of ropes, the rope itself may become the worst threat of all. Thus for a greenhorn, the east face of Moffet held some dangers. For fifty interacting greenhorns the threat appeared to me to be magnified a thousand times for greenhorns and experts alike.

I sidled down to the enlisted quarters and quietly checked the opinions of my trusted 10th Mountain group. They had been in the army long enough to avoid even body language that might suggest opposition to the C.O. ("Whistle blowing" had yet to be invented.) However, their shrugs, their glances toward heaven, the faint smiles of irony, the wrinkled brows, the slaunchwise looks at each other were clear enough answers for me.

One of the likable things about Major Forrest was his openness with the junior officers. He did not expect "yes men" and did not substitute rank for a serious discussion. So at the morning officers' meeting his brow hardly went up at my reaction to the proposal of the day. "I think it's crazy, sir. The instructional team has not yet dealt with such numbers on a dangerous slope. These candidates have no idea yet of what they will be facing. I doubt if they have ever heard of slope failure or collapsing ledges or have ever seen a rock avalanche, much less ever engaged in the lively sport of dodging rocks that whistle and sing and bounce and buzz as they go by. I think that the chances of injury and death on that slope at this stage are quite high."

I was aware of my own possible overreaction. The memory of the flowery ledge that dropped out from under us, leaving us hanging by our fingers on a 100-foot sheer cliff, was and always will be fresh and vivid. The other junior officers at the meeting had been there, remembered, and said nothing. Major Forrest had not had that experience, but I'm not certain that it would have changed him much. For him danger seemed to be a source of stimulus and excitement.

> I see what you mean, but there are other points to be considered. First is that war is loaded with hazards, injuries, and fatalities. At what point do we who train stop playing games and start toughening up? Second, it's hard to learn about the treachery of Aleutian slopes without getting out on them. We can talk forever, but the learning starts when the rocks begin to whistle. Why not Thursday? The men will all be wearing helmets. That should help. The third point has nothing directly to do with mountaineering. We are under pressure to produce a cadre of teachers to train a task force a few months down the road. We simply won't have the luxury time that the 10th Mountain Infantry had. They took two years starting with the best mountaineers in the nation. We have half a year starting with minimally trained mountaineers except for us in NPCS. Some of the education may well end up being a simple matter of physical survival of the course in the allotted time. But what's wrong with that? Isn't a man who has learned rapidly how to survive a rugged situation apt to be a good teacher in the art of survival?

Well, we could see that, whatever the course of wisdom, the mass attack by amateurs on the east face of Mt. Moffet was going to take place. I got back to the MTG boys and we started to lay out a plan that would separate the class into manageable groups and keep them far enough apart laterally on the slope to minimize the danger of rock falling from above. We also tried to keep the climbing route on the spurs. Dislodged rocks tend to follow gullies. "Tend" is a key word. There are also those rocks that bounce out of the gullies and ricochet around in more interesting trajectories. The major was to lead the climb. The junior officers would keep track of things at the trailing edge where trouble was most apt to show up or end up. The schedule called for a late afternoon assembly on a large swale below the summit where we would all bivouac for the night. This meant, of course, that the men would be carrying fairly heavy packs—an additional hazard to a greenhorn on a tricky slope. I'm sure the MTG gang had crossed its collective fingers and breathed a collective prayer for a liberal benediction of luck as we dismounted from the trucks early Thursday morning and started up the gentle, lumpy incline leading toward the east face of Mt. Moffet.

I say "lumpy incline," but actually we were advancing up a tongue of moraine left by an ancient glacier. The lumps were huge boulders dumped in place by the ice as it melted back. Associated with the lumps were pockets in the moraine called "kettleholes" where buried ice blocks had melted out. These became small ponds which were now overgrown, hidden and disguised by a thick mat of floating vegetation. An uninitiated foot soldier might first be amused by the rolling elastic footing he was experiencing, and then become amazed and thoroughly initiated by falling through the mat into icy black muck. A few of our party were thus educated and the rest educated by association when we helped them out. In due time we became ecologists to the extent of recognizing the indicator vegetation for muskeg. Ah, yes, muskeg. I now had cause to recall General Buckner's secret orders giving birth to NPCS in which he mandated training in "muskeg combat," a term he did not define. NPCS had now discovered muskeg. Before another sun had risen, six of us would have developed a good working definition for "muskeg combat."

A morning of heavy trudging and the morainal valley ended against a couple of hundred feet of scree slope leading up to the base of the 500-foot cliffs of the east face. The whole rugged scene was softened by vegetational greenery. Short grasses struggled up through the scree; long grasses padded the steps and gentler slopes of the face. At the bottom of the scree slope we divided our party into five climbing teams, each team led by an MTG noncom, assisted by two or three others from the instructional team. For emergency purposes the instructors carried ropes and first aid packets. Major Forrest went with team 1, climbing the spur farthest to the left. The other teams were distributed among the spurs to the right. Captain Krause, as rear guard, was to my left and Lieutenant Hitchcock to my right. "Here we go," murmured a voice too soft to be heard. It was mine.

The five climbing teams were strung across the entire east face. Everything was progressing well, though a little too slowly. In October at this latitude night comes early and the east face is far from ideal for night climbing. The teams were sticking to the spurs because death by cannonade lurked in the gulches. Sir Edward Whymper in his famous "Scrambles amongst the Alps" coined the word "cannonade" to express his feeling for rockfall. There is no better word. I should add here that years ago, a teenager on the face of Fin Dome in the Sierra Nevada, I almost killed myself in needless panic over a falling rock. Since then I just watch warily and dodge when necessary. It has worked quite well so far.

At this time I was rear guard in the middle, in close touch with Team 3 but keeping my right eye on Team 4. Way to my left, considerably higher and moving right along, was Team 1 and Major Forrest. They were almost out of the trouble zone and closing in on the bivouac site. Team 4 was moving out of my direct sight onto the far side of their spur. Once I looked across the gulch and saw a candidate apparently hung up in a tight situation, unable to move. But his team leader was getting a rope to him. All looked okay, so my attention came back to Team 3. It needed it. The lad at the head was getting too frisky, flitting around, jumping gaps, not paying attention to the rotten footing these cliffs specialize in.

Rock fall was fairly constant but was usually preceded by the warning, "Rock!"—a moment of tension and then back to the business of climbing. Suddenly, on the far side of the spur to my right, I heard a yell and heavy crunch as a big chunk of ledge let go. I saw pieces of it explode out into the air. Then I saw a rucksack take flight, spinning so furiously that socks, canteen, rations and utensils flew out by centrifugal force. "Some guy is going to have a long, lonesome climb for his equipment," I thought. While I was thinking that thought another rucksack whirled out into view amid more rock fragments. I watched with growing horror as I realized it was not a rucksack.

Check first aid kit! Get rappel rope out and into action! Yell at the leaders of Teams 3 and 4 to freeze the men in place, turning off the rock shower! Rappel like mad back down to the scree slope! Run and slide the rest of the way to where the unlucky candidate had stopped rolling after almost 400 feet of flying, whirling, flopping and bouncing like a rag doll. He had to be dead. No one could take a beating like that and live. No one, that is, except this tough Paiute Native American. As I skidded over the grassy scree to his side he was groaning softly "Oh me. Oh me." His scalp had a ragged gash and of course the wind had been pounded out of him, but I had hope when he moved both arms and legs for me.

MTG's Toni Matt, Ernest Tapley and Bill Bowes came leaping down to help, followed shortly by Lt. Harry Hitchcock. Our Paiute could probably never in the world have found a team better suited to the rescue assignment ahead. He was lying on a steep scree slope at least four miles from the nearest phone or help. That was four miles of heavy tundra hummocks, boulders, gorges, streams, and muskeg. Incredibly, Tapley was back in two hours, bounding up the slope with those spring steel legs, carrying a heavy litter on his shoulders as though it were a fly rod. He, too, was Native American, at least in part. Perhaps there was an ancient bond at work that night.

It was black night before we began to move. The lack of voices and falling rock from above suggested that the rest of the gang had made it to the bivouac site and were even now sacked out. Our assignment was just beginning. The injured candidate, we discovered, weighed 230 pounds stripped. He wasn't stripped.

The routine for the retreat called for four litter bearers, and one "rester" on belay to the rear or searching the route ahead. We stumbled, grunted, sweated, and rotated. One rotation I recall took place unplanned. I was on the left rear handle of the litter. Toni Matt was on the right. In the dark I suddenly plopped into a muskeg hole. Toni reached over and grabbed my handle without dropping his. The caravan moved ahead without a hitch, glitch, or sag. Lt. Harry Hitchcock snaked me out of the muck and rushed ahead to take my place on the litter while I tried to shake off the goo without loosing contact with the parade.

In this way we ground along, getting closer and closer to exhaustion without actually collapsing. A little after two o'clock in the morning we slipped the litter and its passenger into the waiting ambulance. Then we lay down on the tundra near the road and went to sleep, hardly noting the light rain that had commenced. When I awoke about noon the next day I felt as though someone had clubbed me all over with a 2 x 4. Toni was sitting up grinning at me and my muddy costume.

Odds and Ends: In addition to broken ribs, punctured lung, cuts and bruises, the injured man had sustained a skull fracture that later cost him the sight in one eye. He was returned to the states, hospitalized, and discharged. It was a big rock that had knocked him off the cliff while he was in the act of putting on his rucksack. In addition to pure luck and his own tough fiber, he owed his life to two major factors. First was his helmet which deflected a rock that would have caved in his skull. Second were the tundra cushions that bounced him from one ledge to the next without bashing him to pieces.

The rest of the party all survived in good style their first big day and night in the mountains. Of course I was loaded with unmentionable "I—told—you—so's" for the major. However, in later consideration I recalled that, after all, only one man had been injured. None had been killed. That was certainly not the holocaust of my worst scenario. I suspect all of us, candidates and instructional staff alike, had had what is now called a learning experience.

And from it, we had a multiple definition of muskeg combat: (1) Combat against muskeg; (2) Individual or group defensive

Autumn color, Shagak Bay background

measures against muskeg entrapment, especially at night; (3) Various antics for extricating one's self from the aromatic black muck of muskeg.

Autumn

Autumn color, autumn breezes.
Horizontal rain that freezes.
Days are shorter. Nights are longer.
Homesick soldiers' spirits flounder.
The men are soaked. The tents are flat.
A williwaw is where we're at.
It's undermining heart and soul!
Let's take 'em out on night patrol.

With no trees on Adak, we were unprepared for the display of autumn color that sneaked up on us. It started with the leaves of geranium and wild rhubarb that suddenly turned bright red. Then, of all things, the grasses moved with deliberation from Irish green to bright yellows and orange, to a rich red brown with streaks of magenta, before fading away to old straw. The sun was low on the horizon so the illuminating colors were those of early morning and evening. With the addition of moving cloud shadows, there was something both incandescent and kaleidoscopic at work on the Aleutian landscape. Had we known our nation's history a little better we would have been less amazed at the grassland colors of Adak. The native grasses of the U.S. prairie states are very colorful in autumn. In the last 200 years, noncolorful European grasses have replaced the native grasses almost as completely as Europeans have replaced the Native Americans.

The weather's fundamental autumnal trend toward increasing violence was camouflaged somewhat by considerable shifting to and fro. Aleutian air always seems to be hurrying somewhere. The most overworked cartoon about Aleutian wind shows soldiers standing around with a built-in lean. One morning Sergeant Niss and I infused life and realism into the cartoon. Prior to morning roll call, in secrecy, we trained our whole company to snap to attention with a prominent lean to the right. So when the major bawled "TEN—HUT!" we had the pleasure of watching a disgraceful failure in West Point discipline.

Even with the meteorological ups and downs, we developed an automatic response to the signs of a savage autumn squall coming our way. When, off to the west or southwest, we saw, among all the dark clouds a blacker cloud wearing long filmy gray skirts that swept the sea or land surface, we took immediate defense measures. Get out the parka or any other foul weather gear. Zip up, tie down, pull the pucker strings, protect face, especially eyes, get off the ridge, hunker down behind a boulder, back to the wind. In a few minutes, it is past. Outer clothes are probably wet through or coated with frozen slush. Any patch of skin left exposed may be stinging sufficiently to increase efficiency next time. From the general buffeting, you may realize that had you been caught unwary on the ridge, you might have gotten bucked off. The chief difference between these squalls and those equally ferocious Midwest midsummer storms in the lower forty-eight was the absence of thunder and lightning in the Aleutians.

Most of our weather came out of the west or southwest where the enemy lived and our meteorologists did not. Hence we rarely had much advance warning. One morning we woke up early to the deep bass music of our vibrating cabin. A Wagnerian-sized storm was moving in. From the window overlooking Kuluk Bay, we could see that horizontality was the theme. From the tall grasses now quivering and flat around the cabin to the clouds streaming rapidly along the mountainside across the bay, everything was responding to a vast horizontal driving force. The surface of the bay itself had been torn loose and was now a deep layer of spume hiding all but the masts and funnels of the warships straining at their mooring cables. Once in a while a box or ragged sheet of plywood would sail through our field of vision and disappear.

Since none of the three officers in our cabin had had any prior experience with such a monster, we were torn between curiosity of the unknown and the caution of ignorance. Finally I couldn't stand it any longer. With sketch pad and pencil I wrestled my way through the front door out onto the tundra. I was standing a hundred feet above the bay and the air was liberally seasoned with salt. It was hard to stand or move against the wind but I finally found a snug hollow among the hummocks and sat down to watch and sketch.

In a strange way we were partially sheltered from the full blast. The wind was blowing generally toward the cliff. Most of the airstream was directed by the cliff into a roaring updraft. For a limited distance back from the edge there was a strip of relative calm.

As I glanced around the countryside, I could see no sign of life. No people strolling around in town. No dogs skulking in the streets and alleys. No birds flying. They'd have been stripped of their feathers and ready for the pot. Did I say no birds?

A pair of ravens came flying low over the tundra, bucketing around in the turbulence. Their feathers looked as though they hadn't had any preening for a month. Either they were bent on suicide or they just didn't give a damn because they were headed directly into the invisible sheet of 100 mph updraft at the edge of the cliff. I watched them sail casually into the sheet and get blasted into the sky, end over end, flopping helplessly, losing a feather or two as they went. In a few seconds they were a couple of black dots aloft, dead or alive, speeding downwind in the general direction from which they came. In a few minutes they returned, looking more scruffy than ever, and did it again. Do ravens ever get killed in their daredeviltry? What is the reason for this behavior? It certainly didn't look as though it had any survival value. If they were trying to show off, I wasn't much of an audience although I was deeply impressed.

Some time later, back at the cabin I found my two colleagues a bit anxious and restless. Some contrapuntal music had been added to the bass melody of the cabin. There were whistles and squeaks as of rusty twenty-penny nails yielding bit by bit. There

Autumn squall coming

Shagak camp is born

were cracking noises as of—well—something cracking, percussion noise as of something loose, slatting in the breeze. The wind had shifted and now seemed to be blowing in a direction that might drag the cabin off its foundation and dump it over the cliff.

Altogether this seemed like a good moment to seek other shelter. That thought was punctuated as we caught sight of an outhouse bounding over the tundra, trying to get airborne before going over the cliff. "I hope it's not occupied," said Harry Hitchcock as it disappeared over the edge. Without bothering to pack we donned our foul weather gear and erupted out onto the tundra.

The major joined us and we fought the blast into town, looking for better shelter and curious to see the extent of the damage. "Not too much," seemed to be the general opinion. A few power poles were down. Several Quonset huts had large dents from unidentified flying objects. One Quonset had lost its roof. The occupants located it not too far away, wrapped around the base of a water tank. A couple of small boats and one aircraft were said to be "totaled." It was rumored that a man had been killed, almost cut in two by a winged scrap of sheet iron. "Not too bad," they said. That was nice to know. One minor note: I was splattered from head to foot by flying mud sheared off the road by the heavy gusts.

By evening the storm had weakened and we returned to the shelter of our cabins for the night. We now knew why we had been offered such lush accommodations in such a superb setting. Within a couple of days we were relocated in more stable surroundings. But that was just the beginning. Within a week we had located a base camp site on the far side of the pass leading to Shagak Bay. Here, five or six miles from town, beside a small lake, we (staff, students, and a Weasel doing truck duty) erected a village of ten large army wall tents. This would be the main launching pad for the training program. It was closer to the mountains and the storms. It was farther from civilized padding. A ten-mile round-trip hike was far enough to discourage the casually curious and those who like to think they "need to know" but only blot up a lot of precious time. It was near enough for supplies, emergencies, and contact with those who really did need to know. In other words, this looked like the right place.

Oddly enough, Tokyo Rose provided confirmation. She reported, with her usual insults, that the island of Amchitka was the site where 10,000 Alaskan troops were getting mountain combat training by a detachment from the 10th Mountain Division of Colorado. Obviously she was aware of us but, considering her usual accuracy, this was an unbelievable goof. But we made no effort to correct her. (Less than 300 men were being trained by NPCS on Adak. Amchitka has no mountains.) Instead we eased quietly away from town into our low-profile Shagak Camp and embraced the fog.

An Evening with Willi

Shagak Camp was about as comfortable as a military tent camp could be—in the late autumn on an Aleutian island. Though nearly flat, the grassy meadow had just enough slope to give good general drainage in a hard rain. The big military tents had no floor so we dug shallow trenches around the outside perimeter of each tent. A big tent sheds a lot of

Shagak camp after slush storm

water in a rainstorm. These tents were 10' x 10' square pyramids of heavy canvas with a five-foot wall at the bottom for headroom and to prevent snow encroachment. Each tent was supported internally by a single sturdy central pole. Outside were the usual rope loops and guy ropes pegged down by two-foot oak stakes. The wooden pole was topped by a metal cap from which protruded a heavy iron rod. The rod ran loosely through the center hole in a steel washer about the size of a saucer, which in turn was attached to the open apex of the tent by four steel chains. The open apex gave ventilation and allowed space for a stovepipe. When properly mounted and staked down, the tent seemed as solid as a house though perhaps a tad more drafty. However, to make certain that we were Aleutian proof, we added four guy ropes that ran directly from outside stakes to the top of

Bitchin' Ridge

the pole. The tent now was as taut as a kettle drum. A good port in a storm—and we did have a few.

The first days after moving in were spent exploring the nearby mountains for teaching areas. Shagak Camp was partially surrounded by a horseshoe-shaped range of mountains with a saw-bladed crest, subsequently dubbed "Bitchin' Ridge." Early in their mobility training the candidates were introduced to the crest and were required to white-knuckle the three-mile circuit on the cockscomb, preferably without falling or being blasted off by the wind. After all, good candidates are hard to come by.

For reasons unknown to me, a flock of Hepburn's rosy finches was almost always present on that windy crest. The closest call we ever had there occurred on a day of dense fog driven by a sixty-knot breeze. A finch, apparently flying blind, zinged out of the fog and bopped a candidate on the head, knocking him down but not quite off the ridge. His helmet liner accompanied the ruined finch downwind into oblivion. However, it was a stormy night traverse of the ridge that gave birth to its name. Those of us down in Shagak Camp, surrounded by the mountains, could hear the clear angelic voices from heaven above, calling upon their maker, registering comments and complaints every step of the way. So "Bitchin' Ridge" it became and still is, in spite of ignorant modern cartographers.

But I have digressed shamefully. This story really starts when the four NPCS officers, tired from a day of honest labor, crawled into one of the big pyramid tents for our well-earned rest. In seconds we were asleep.

Sometime later I awoke with a jump. Outside there was a monstrous roaring sound rapidly getting more monstrous. "Hey! What's up?" I yelled at Harry Hitchcock next to me. By the time he answered it was difficult to separate voice from uproar and impossible to decode the message. The tent, shaking and slatting with vigor, now began to leap and buck like an impatient rodeo bronco in the chute. Not having any inkling of what had gotten loose on the landscape, I couldn't avoid wondering if our safe haven of canvas had any unsuspected flaws. Now and then I could detect a human voice crying aloud in the wilderness but got no illumination on what was happening at high speed in the blackness outside.

Then, as though someone had switched off the audio, the night was suddenly completely calm and silent—silent, that is, except for the major, who was caught by the sudden silence in the middle of bellowing "IT'S A WILLIWAW!" with such force that I'm sure everyone within a radius of a couple of miles understood clearly and forever that it was a williwaw—whatever that might be. Possibly a species of Jabberwocky, with a big whiffle. In a more subdued voice, the major suggested that we were not out of trouble yet and that it would be advisable to.... His suggestion was cut short by a mighty roar; all of a sudden, Willi was on top of us again, slapping the tent around as though it were a paper bag. There was a vibrant thud, signaling the failure of one of the pegs. Instantly the tent felt looser and the thunder of its flapping increased. I tried to yell a warning but I couldn't even hear my own voice. Again, within seconds the roar subsided. I heard Harry say "Wow" quietly to himself. All had heard the peg go. What next?

A few years before the war, I was camping with family in a light four-man tent in the Quetico when a "June heller" hit. We saved the tent from ripping out and blowing away by shipping the center pole and getting it and us flat on the ground. I proposed now to the officers that before too many pegs pulled out, Harry and I should try to ship the big center pole while the other two stayed clear. The army tent pole was about four inches in diameter and ten feet high. It would probably come down fast and hard enough to brain anyone in its trajectory. I wasn't at all sure Harry and I could even budge it from its footing.

Willi and Hell returned, not the least bit exhausted. All of us heard the thuds as, in rapid sequence, two or three more pegs failed and the tent began to feel its freedom. I slapped Harry on the shoulder. We stood up and grabbed the bouncing pole near its base and heaved. It moved slightly. We took a breath and heaved again. Two more heaves and down came the pole, the tent, and at least two officers. All bounced as they hit the hard ground. The officers were a bit stunned by the blow but the tent and pole now went wild. In the pitch darkness that was no trivial matter. The pole was lashing around as though it were a huge club in the hands of a blind giant. We had to get control of it using the touch system or risk getting made into jelly.

Suddenly peace and quiet again. Harry, Marty Krause, the major and I felt for the pole and took up prone positions on top of it. Once more the roar of the meat grinder. The four of us managed to stay on top of the pole, but it was the roughest ride I've ever had. Furthermore, a new threat had developed. The pole had pulled free from the apex of the tent and no longer exercised any control over the big steel washer and four chains anchoring it to the canvas. These now became a mace and chain in the hands of the blind giant. I could hear the steely hum and whang as this new weapon whipped around in the darkness. A couple of times I felt the breeze as it just missed my skull. Still I dared not let the bucking pole get away again, so I stayed on top and hoped.

At the next pause Marty Krause leaped off the pole, found the entrance to the prone tent and snaked outside shouting something unintelligible. In a few seconds we heard the Weasel's motor start up. It came closer. Marty yelled, "Watch yourselves. I'm coming up on the tent!" We shrunk away from the sound direction. In a few seconds the Weasel was up on an area of the tent where we were not. Marty had managed to pin down both the pole and the mace and chain. The motor died, and Marty was back inside the tent when the curtain went up again.

Marty, you and I were never very close friends, but that evening you sure earned our respect and gratitude forever.

The williwaw bellowed and blasted off and on all night but the tent only rippled heavily but comfortingly over the top of us. Bruised, pounded, battered and exhausted, believe it or not we slept quite well. When we awoke, day was at hand and Willi was gone like a bad dream.

A williwaw is essentially an avalanche of cold, often night air cascading down off a snowy mountain crest. Channeling the draft, as in a deep narrow gorge in the mountainside, may increase the velocity.* Williwaws thus may approximate hurricane velocities. Shagak Camp, lying at the bottom of a bowl created by Bitchin' Ridge, was perhaps prime williwaw territory. I have no explanation for the pulsating rhythm of its attacks.

Willi, being a nocturnal creature, was absent by day but a frequent visitor when we were trying to sleep. However, it was that first night that carried the main message. Center poles are not sufficient support for tents in williwaw territory. Our camp had been completely flattened and a few tents blown away and lost. We sent the Weasel to town for replacements and a few loads of lumber and set to work rebuilding the camp. This time the tents were supported by an internal framework that seemed able to survive williwaws. One day when we were in the tents riding out a typhoon we watched our lumber pile gradually disappear as board after board flipped into the air and sailed away. We were later able to salvage some of the boards from the immediate landscape. I especially remember three two-by-fours driven like arrows four feet deep into the hillside tundra. All these diversions slowed down the official training program but were nevertheless important extracurricular education.

---

* Hurd C. Willett, *Descriptive Meteorology* (New York: Academic Press, Inc., 1944): 259.

Shagak Camp, repairs after tents were flattened by a williwaw

Darkness is a State of Mind

With the willi-proof reconstruction of Shagak Camp, the training program went forward again. The trainees went out on longer and longer cross-country excursions until we all had put foot on most of Adak. The trainees had become used to the precision and delicacy required for living in the two-man mountain tent. They could cook their meals inside the tent over the little one-burner stove without killing themselves with carbon monoxide or setting the tent on fire. Most of them had learned while in the tents to curb those enthusiastic gesticulations that sometimes swat the kettle and serve soup all over the walls and sleeping bags. In the middle of a night snowstorm they could exit the tent on bodily errands and usually find their way back without waking their buddies with stentorian requests for guidance. They could get all their gear repacked inside the knapsack the next morning instead of having to tie some of it outside in the rain.

Most of the men had learned how to use a compass to get to some particular place in a storm and to estimate their travel time to get there on schedule. Considering that all these soldiers had had some compass and map training before coming to us, this last item proved to be more difficult than I thought it should until I discovered a common mental glitch. One night when we had all the squads out on separate night marching missions, I placed myself at a crossroads where all must pass sometime so that I could check them out. One squad came trudging along, the leader with compass in hand. I stopped him and asked "What azimuth are you following?" He answered immediately "130 degrees, sir." It was a clear night and since we had given a little star training, I asked him, "Can you point out the North Star?" He scanned the sky and then, "That's it there," pointing to a star lying in the direction they had just been traveling, azimuth 130 degrees. I was completely nonplussed but said nothing for a moment while I tried to figure out what went wrong. Then I asked, "Could you point the approximate direction to Chicago?" Now he was stunned. He shook his head, looking at me as though I'd pitched him an unfair curved ball. So I asked in another way, "We are here on Adak, and you've seen maps of North America. Could you tell me roughly in your own words where Chicago lies from here?" "Well," he said, "it's sorta southeast I guess." "OK," I said, "now look at your North Star and point about where Chicago lies." He wrestled with that and finally pointed. "Now," I said, "look at your compass carefully and show me where Chicago should be." After a little study he pointed, correctly, approximately in the direction he had been walking (which was also in the direction he had chosen for his North Star). I said, "You have given me two completely different directions to Chicago. What's wrong?"

Well, he finally worked it through, but before that night was over I had discovered that this young man was by no means the only one for whom "azimuth" was only a number, not a way of sensing one's position in the world. Thereafter every time we started a hike, or made camp, or paused for a breather, I asked, "Where's Chicago?" (or Japan, or the South Pole) until they all could give me reasonable answers from the compass, or sun, or stars, or even a distant view of Mt. Moffet. Later, if the visibility was good, I could ask without warning, "What is our position on the map?" with the expectation that at least someone in each squad could find it. If that person was not the squad leader, the man who spotted it correctly became leader of that squad pro tem. Night, fog, and snowstorms could cause disorientation. Our goal was to create a team that could navigate overland, by map, compass, and clock. Beneath that goal was the more urgent one of doing the same for the officers and instructors of NPCS. The Aleutians were putting us all to the test with no respect for rank.

I remember too well one foggy night we designated the summit of a prominent knoll on the south side of Mt. Moffet as a midnight rendezvous for four squads starting from different points, each about five miles from the knoll. My parting words were, "This is to be a night of stealth. No shouting, no talking, no use of light except held under cover to check map, compass, or watch. Try to arrive at the crest of the knoll some time between quarter of twelve and twelve o'clock. At quarter after twelve the problem is over. Those of you not there can finish with the help of vocal signals. I'll be waiting for you with my clock and little black book. Any questions?"

Sad to say, at quarter of twelve I had not yet found the knoll. I knew the snowpack had slowed me, but even so. "Damn!" I said, silently of course, and started to search, laterally, first to the right and then to the left, searching farther with each zig. Once when I stopped to breathe and ponder I heard, off there in the black to the right, muffled speech and the soft trudging of boots in snow. Hurrying to the right again, my feet told me of steepening slope. The knoll! I scrambled, panting to the summit. The first squad was already there looking around. It was now ten minutes after twelve. Luckily I got in the first words, "Where have you guys been? I've been looking all over the knoll for you!" That was close!

We waited a few minutes. None of the other three squads had arrived by 12:15, when we gave the "view halloo." From three different directions we received answers out of the opacity of the Aleutian night.

Lesson: Don't dream up problems you can't do yourself unless you want to test yourself.

The Battle for Allusive Clothing. Phase I

"How in hell do we get dry, walking around in the rain?" That laconic question, issuing from a nearby mountain tent in the middle of a November night and audible over the roar of one of our horizontal rainstorms, rang a gong deeper than the question and pushed me to face a serious dilemma. We were in the middle of a survival and mobility test that we had been working up to for some time. As usual everyone, candidates and instructors alike, were going to be well tested.

The starting point was our Adak quarters, where we were taking a weekend break after a couple of weeks at Shagak Camp. With no warning to the class, we routed everyone out of his warm sleeping bag at 12:01 A.M. of a stormy Monday with orders to pack for a three-day reconnaissance and rendezvous. The disbelief on the faces of the candidates would have made a great class picture. To tell the truth, I'd have been delighted to drop the whole thing there, indulge in a good laugh, and send everyone back to his sack. But there was nothing in the major's face that suggested any deviation from the assignment as stated.

The gang was divided up into three night reconnaissance groups, each under the leadership of one NPCS officer. "Reconnaissance" was a fancy title for traversing a given route at night in a hellish rainstorm. This would occupy the best part of two nights followed by a half day to reach the rendezvous point, a cove on the west coast. "Rendezvous time," said the major, "will be noon Wednesday. If you arrive early and I am not there, wait until noon, then leave a message on the stake at the top of the bluff above the cove and return to Adak Base and report in. I will stay at the cove until 1:00 P.M., at which time the assignment ends. At that time, wherever you are, turn back to Adak Base and report in on arrival. Any questions?"

Shaky voice in the dark: "Yeah, what do we do if we have bad trouble or something on the way?"

Major: "Do whatever makes sense. Any other questions? O.K. I'll expect to see you all at noon on Wednesday at the cove. Good luck."

The Cove, Adak 1945

The sound of splashing feet and rain drumming on the parka hood drowned out the mutterings. NPCS et al. melted into the maelstrom.

Along with the testing of men against the elements there was, riding on this jaunt in the dark, a test of clothing for Aleutian soldiers. Most of us had been wearing and carrying the gear we arrived with when we joined NPCS at Dutch Harbor. Summer had been gentle with us but the horizontal rains of autumn called loudly for change. Adak's supply lines were quite adequate for those who could retreat to a Quonset hut to warm up and dry out, or could reach for a rain suit hanging in the closet. But those supply lines showed little consideration for men who worked in the mountains and carried everything from shelter and food to arms and ammunition on their backs.

Nevertheless, we made some important gains, thanks to the major. He discovered that all-rubber shoepacs were available, and found a cobbler who had a supply of rubber-cleated soles he could attach to the boots. Not only did we now have good footwear for wet mountains but by tying our water-repellent pant legs tightly around the boot we could skip dry shod through the many small streams—as long as the water was less than waist deep. A regular waterproof infantry field outfit did not exist, but by borrowing a few navy rain suits we could test out the problems of day to day living with waterproof outer garments. In short, we discovered that by adjusting the inner garments, perspiration became much less of a threat than rain water oozing through water-repellent outer gear. I will freely admit that the extreme case of a bare torso under a rubber jacket in a cold rain is an unforgettable experience in clammy sensations, but it was not lethal and it was nice to have a dry shirt and undershirt in the knapsack ready to deliver comfort when needed. It looked as though waterproofing our men in autumn was worth a field test.

Some time in early October the major fired off a request to the Office of Quartermaster General (OQMG) in Washington, D.C., explaining our predicament, our preliminary tests and our needs. In a couple of weeks, fifty new uniforms arrived for testing and report. They were exactly what we had ordered—except they were not waterproof. The accompanying letter explained that after a preliminary test at Ft. Belvoir, Virginia, OQMG had substituted water-repellent fabric because of excessive perspiration. We groaned in misery. How do we explain to D.C. that Ft. Belvoir is not Adak? However, the uniforms looked to be well designed and well made. The sturdy poplin

Difficult terrain at night

appeared to have a tight weave, so we decided to introduce the uniforms to the test at hand. As we left Adak Base and slogged south into the teeth of a November storm, most of us were wearing the new test uniform.

My group's route took us around the west end of Kuluk Bay and Sweeper Cove to Finger Bay, then south past a cirque lake, to a low gap in the headwall, and finally west to the north shore of Bay of Islands. That was the end of the required night work. From there we would follow the shore west and north to the rendezvous cove and finally overland back to base. I had already been over most of the area at one time or another, but under the circumstances of that night, after we had left the roads and tracks of the naval base, the view in all directions was opaque jet. The only familiar items were compass, clock, and flashlight. We wrestled with the hummocks and the lashing wind. We stumbled, wallowed, fell through tundra roofs that had grown over deep little stream channels. We made many rest stops and head counts. The footing improved when we entered the valley occupied by Finger Bay. The bay itself was not visible, but we turned south up the valley and in due time found ourselves walking the shore of the lake.

Although still night, it seemed like an excellent time and place for a sodden, exhausted gang to bivouac. Time to get under cover before chill set in. It is likely that our group had achieved a new military record for low-velocity marching: approximately one mile per hour. That in itself is a good index of the energy cost for that first leg of the march.

With a liberal expenditure of our remaining energy, we finally nailed down all the tents before they sailed away forever into the night. I was a little jumpy until the bodies were inside the tents. Mountain tents don't fly well when loaded with bodies. At last I was in my own tent. What a relief to have that tough thin fabric between me and the atmospheric pounding outside. First item was to get the little one-burner gasoline stove into action. Within a few minutes the tent was warm. My new improved uniform was soaked through. My shirt and undershirt were quite wet. It felt good to get them off and start soaking up some fresh heat. After a big mug of hot stew I stripped down and hung the clothes from the tent apex to dry, rolled out my sleeping bag, doused the stove and climbed in. As I drifted off I remembered that we had pitched the tents on the only relatively flat area and it was fairly squashy. Well, the floor was waterproof. Wasn't it?

Day was well under way when I awoke. Our plan was to wait until 3:30 P.M. to start the last leg of our night work. If we packed swiftly and moved out at that time, we might still have enough daylight for visible footing on the far side of the pass. As heard from my sleeping bag, the storm outside seemed as vigorous as ever. Then I became conscious of a fine cold mist settling on my face. The outside cover of the sleeping bag was wet. Everything in the tent was wet. The clothes I had hung up to dry were wringing wet. Yesterday's socks had not been very wet when I removed them but they certainly were soaked now. It seems the force of the wind was powerful enough to blast the rain right through the aging waterproof tent fabric.

There was also a substantial puddle on the floor that had soaked everything piled there, including the bottom of my sleeping bag. Was the puddle only accumulated mist or was it in part water oozing up from the soggy ground? Take a chance. With an eating fork I gently forced the tines through the floor cloth and had the pleasure of watching the water drain slowly out through the four small holes. Pure luck.

With the stove going the tent felt warm, and I had a hot breakfast. But with the incoming mist the wet clothing was not drying. There was not enough fuel to run the stove all day. For a moment I paused to consider the implications of this development. Then the moment was overridden by the need to make rounds and check the men. Saving my dry clothes for emergency, I donned yesterday's wet ones and ducked out into a storm now spiced up with a few snowflakes.

At 3:30 the group was packed and ready. Under their parka hoods most faces displayed noncommittal durability. A few smiled wryly. A few looked a bit stony. We were off for the pass, a few hundred vertical feet of unspectacular but slippery muddy climbing. Being able to use the last of the daylight allowed us to move faster and more accurately. By the time black night fell, we were well over the pass and nearly down to the little stream flowing toward Bay of Islands. Before midnight we had reached a small lake on the north shore of the bay. While the rest pitched tents, one of the NPCS noncoms and I walked a stretch of the shore to see if there was enough driftwood to make a bonfire.

That was a crazy hope. It hit me when I watched the sluggishness of the men as they dropped their packs and moved to pitch tents. Fortunately we didn't find any driftwood or we might have wasted more time trying to fire it in that storm. My own tent pitching was not a model of military snap and precision. I felt dull and tired; chill was beginning to affect my motions. I remember barking an angry order at my hands to stop shaking so I could get the stove going without burning the tent down. It worked.

The warmth of the stove reduced the shakes, and I went ahead with the routine chores of getting a hot supper, peeling off the wet clothes (that meant everything I was wearing), trying to give them a chance to dry out a little. Tomorrow I would have to wear the remaining dry set even though they would be under the still wet field jacket and trousers. How long would they stay dry? I kept the stove going as long as I dared. After all, in terms of distance we were about half way through the exercise. Daylight travel should be easier but to what extent would this be offset by the condition of the men—and me?

I turned the sleeping bag inside out to at least warm its now damp interior. When I turned the stove off and climbed in I was aware again of the wind-driven bursts of cold mist taking over. Damn! It was about this time that I heard the question coming from the nearest tent. "How in hell do we get dry walking around in the rain?" There was immediate response from the other tents. "Yeah. What are we learning from this exercise?" "How can we fight the Japs if we've already been bumped off by the weather?" etc., etc. Any one who had something to say said it loudly and clearly. Mutiny? Maybe. Desperation? Possibly.

Was it serendipity or accident that we were camped at the near end of a relatively easy shortcut to the base? If we took the rendezvous route all shortcuts would be blocked by Bitchin' Ridge. On the other hand, the major had given an order and I was responsible for getting the group to the rendezvous and on time. The major believed in the power of a military order. The major was unhappy with noncourageous leaders who failed to follow through. But I was also responsible for proper care of the men. My pulse was up a bit with the quandary. The two routes were there. I knew about them. I had to decide. Leaning out of the tent door, I shouted, "O.K., O.K., I got your message. We'll have a powwow at daylight. Now stay as dry as you can till then."

The rest of this tale is necessarily brief, mostly because, in spite of strong feelings about it, real memories are sketchy or nonexistent. When the group assembled in the morning, I took one look at the desperate faces and the chattering teeth and my decision was made—especially since my own teeth were chattering. "I am considering a shortcut back to base. Seven or eight miles and a pass, slightly higher than last night's, will get us there. As you know the military game is not democratic but I would be willing to hear comment." A few subdued cheers and a panorama of blue-lipped half-smiles. "O.K. Are there any nays?" None. You don't lightly countermand a superior officer's orders, but, "I now order you to go directly back to base and do what you have to do to stop chattering your damn teeth. It's bad manners. I'll need a strong loyal person to be file closer so we don't lose anyone en route. Any volunteers?" There were, and we were off.

I recall watching my feet moving endlessly on and on. My next memory is of being alone in the hut at base, shaking so badly I was afraid I would never get the oil stove started. First I forgot to turn on the little valve feeding oil to the burner. That cost me a hat full of matches and many minutes of panic. Then there was a cloud of black, greasy, evil-smelling smoke rolling out of the stove. Somehow finally it was functioning. There was heat without the smoke. For perhaps an hour I hovered over the stove, shivering violently. Then gradually the shivering died down and my brain got back in gear.

The other junior officers came in soaked and shivering, ready to hug the stove. Finally the major arrived. He looked at me without smiling. "Where were you?" he asked. I told him, ending with, "At least I did follow your suggestion that when in trouble, do whatever makes sense." Once more he looked intently at me and then left without comment. Since he never mentioned it again, I presume he understood even if he didn't sympathize.

That stormy excursion was and still is a unique experience in my life. It brought the threat of wet, cold and wind chill right to the doorstep. In retrospect, I suppose that our group was looking at the leading edge of hypothermia. In the last few years hypothermia has become recognized as an important killer. How close was my group to deep trouble? One experience can't be rated as much perspective. But diminished physical skills and mental acuity can't be considered a pro survival development.

Kuluk Bay and Adak Town from Mt. Moffet

From a military standpoint it was a shock to realize that we instructors in NPCS had not yet solved the November survival-mobility problem beyond two or three days in the field at a stretch. Maybe by further honing our skills and physical durability we could extend that a little, but not much. We were already in pretty good shape. No, the desperate candidate whose voice cut through the night and storm had asked the right question. Our mountain training, our special tactics and weaponry could all be rendered useless in battle without the right outer clothing.

The World War II history of clothing for U.S. infantry in the Aleutians is not exactly a sparkling record. In the Battle of Attu at least a substantial part of the infantry arrived with clothing more appropriate for a temperate semiarid area. The result was

Major Frank Forrest. C.O. of NPCS

more injury to our men from the wet, cold weather than from the Japanese. Trench foot (renamed "Attu Foot") and hypothermia led to skin lesions, fever, gangrene, exhaustion, unconsciousness, and even death. Such a planning error is interesting in view of an event that took place in October of 1942, several months before the Battle of Attu.

A Maj. Robert Bolling sought out and secretly questioned well-known Alaskan naturalist, Olaus Murie, concerning the Aleutian Islands. That little chat lasted over a week. The major was interested in everything about the islands but especially the weather, terrain, vegetation and the clothing, footwear, and other

Checking snow conditions

Sun up on our company en route across the island after first snow

gear necessary for survival in the field. There was probably no person better equipped to answer Major Bolling's barrage of questions. In the middle 1930s Dr. Murie had made a two-year study of the fauna of the Aleutians and in the process had visited every major island in the chain.

As the conversation went on day after day, Margaret Murie was busy typing up the record. At the end of the quiz Major Bolling gathered up all the typed papers and left with the stated intent of hand carrying it directly to General Buckner. In retrospect this interview was clearly in anticipation of the Attu-Kiska battles. What happened? Did the papers get lost in transit or in the overloaded files at Alaskan headquarters? Even two years after the battle of Attu there was no evidence in Adak that Olaus Murie's voice had been heard. And here we were at NPCS trying, in effect, to train a task force to crash the Kurils—in the equivalent of the altogether.

Allusive Clothing Phase II: Enter Mr. Ford

It's fifty years since World War II. We have been forging ahead on fabrics that can make outdoor life tolerable in places like the Aleutians even in autumn and winter. To most Americans today, Goretex, its relatives and associated fabrics are just part of the scenery. Not to me. Aleutian weather has left me with two prominent reflexes. One is an overwhelming feeling of coziness and security when I sit at home in front of an oak fire and listen to the roar of a whopping rainstorm pounding on the roof. The other is a strange mix of envy and pleasure when I don my modern foul weather suit and saunter out into the storm. Envy that we had no such fabric in the Aleutians when it was urgently needed. Pleasure that we played a part, however small, in the research that helped bring such fabrics into existence. Don't look for bylines or citations. We were in the guinea pig battalion way out on the fringe, taking the meteorological beating. When we squealed, we were hurting. When we grunted, all was well. We did make suggestions, tested gear, and submitted reports to OQMG and prayed. Fortunately some improvements were actually made during the life of NPCS. But it was years before we saw Goretex and the modern lightweight camping gear that rolls so easily off the sporting goods counters today.

Meanwhile, back in 1944 on Adak, the major and I took another swing at the Office of Quartermaster General in Washington, D.C. We wrote a report on the performance of the new uniforms during that wet, cold reconnaissance and asked again for the privilege of testing waterproof fabric. We concluded with the suggestion that a three-day maximum survival period for our troops in the field would put us at a serious disadvantage in combat. Stepping outside military channels (sometimes risky), I wrote a personal letter to Maj. Bob Bates at OQMG. Bob was well known in mountaineering circles. We had met on several occasions when he was working so effectively to equip the 10th Mountain Division for battle. If anyone could help us, Bob was the man. I learned much later that he never received my letter. He was with the 10th Mountain Division in Italy checking on the effectiveness of their gear in actual combat.

There was now a quiet but anxious period of waiting during which we tried to guess what, if anything, was happening in D.C. We never could have guessed what actually did happen. One January morning, out of the eternal fog strode a tall, Lincolnesque gentleman with a knapsack riding on one shoulder. Unlike anyone else on Adak, he was wearing civilian outing clothes. "Hi, I'm from the Office of Quartermaster General and I'm looking for the North Pacific Combat School." Enter Mr. Jim Ford, senior design specialist for the Observation Section of the Research and Development Branch of the Military Planning Division of OQMG, Army Service Forces, Washington, D.C. Whatever the details of his mission, Jim Ford's sudden presence was a very satisfying indication that we had caught the attention of D.C. and that serious action on our request had begun.

Jim was on a circuitous route back to D.C. after having been on maneuvers at McKinley Park, checking the performance of military gear under extreme arctic cold, dry conditions. He would be with us for a month in our subarctic wet, cold climate studying, evaluating and reporting on all our gear, clothing of course, but also rations, vehicles, weapons, tools, and emergency equipment. He would help us with new designs, experiments, tests, and reports. When he departed he would take all the reports and recommendations back to OQMG. There he would supervise the fabrication of the equipment from beginning to completion. Then he would personally accompany the new Aleutian gear back to Adak to see how it all turned out.

That was the intent, and surprisingly enough that is what happened. In fact things started to happen fast. I have little idea how Jim's profession, American archeologist with the Museum of Natural History in New York, qualified him for his military assignment of design specialist for OQMG. Perhaps the linkage was no more than the fact that as a field scientist he had learned a good deal about outdoor survival and getting his work done under rugged conditions. He was a sharp observer and recorder whose notebook at the end of the day was crammed with observations, ideas, sketches, and thoughts. In the evening he would translate the jumble for his journal, which became the basis for reports and recommendations to OQMG.

In the field Jim was an able, thoughtful, and thoroughly delightful companion. His pack rested easily on his broad back. His long legs traversed a lot of tundra without hurrying or tiring. Once in a while the archaeologist broke out when his keen eye spotted a small mound in the landscape that turned out to be an ancient Aleut midden, or a depression that revealed an early Aleut dwelling. At such a time we would feel less like pioneers walking a fresh new land and more like just another wave of restless humans carving new initials in the ancient tundra.

From the time he strolled into NPCS until the end of his stay, Jim was with us in the thick of all activities, from night scrambles in the screaming wind along the cockscomb of Bitchin' Ridge to rock climbing in a wet snowstorm, from testing Major Forrest's inventions (portable Weasel bridge and packboard litter sled) to tasting our delectable native emergency rations. By departure time, probably no one knew NPCS any better than Jim.

Most important, at least from my viewpoint, was that Jim Ford had arrived already sympathetic to our desire for a fair test of waterproof uniforms. His chief worry about them, which I shared, was that in the life-or-death demands of combat or in periods of intense fatigue, many men might not have the time or discipline to go through the cumbersome routine of removing outer clothes, adjusting inner clothes, replacing outer clothes. We discussed at some length the possibility of reducing perspiration by building into the outer jacket ventilation apertures sheltered from rain by overlapping flaps. We even got as far as making sketches to show how and where it could be done. Finally Jim agreed that a waterproof uniform was worth a try. He would have some samples to test on his return from D.C.

Then Jim proceeded to drop a small bomb. It seems there was a new fabric called Jo-cloth (or oxford cloth) that might change the whole concept of waterproof clothing. It was not yet available in quantity and was very expensive, but those factors can change. The Research and Development Branch was experimenting with it and were excited. Jo-cloth was apparently a little like the old canvas duck my father wore when hunting. "The fabric is more pliable than duck and far superior to duck in its porosity when dry and imperviousness when wet. But Jo-cloth has yet to be tested in the field. Now it just so happens that I have with me a half dozen Jo-cloth uniforms. Do you suppose we might give them a proper field test before I return to D.C? This would in no way replace your waterproof clothing test but Jo-cloth is a possible competing candidate—if we get lucky." I could only think of one word, "Wow!"

The Jo-cloth test started right away. In fact, I had hardly said "Wow!" when there was the major in his new uniform standing under a small waterfall. After a few minutes he stepped out fairly dry. What wetness he encountered was caused by splashing. The rest of us tested the suits as opportunities presented themselves. The most common test came when we waded the creeks. With our pants legs tied down snugly around the boot tops, we no longer skipped across the stream. We took our time, splashed

Proposed combat uniform for North Pacific area. These sketches accompanied Jim Ford's report to OQMG. Reproduced at National Archives and declassified June 4, 1992 by NARA.

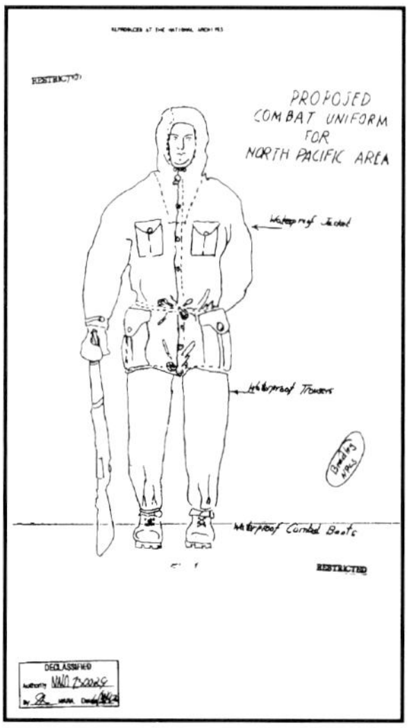

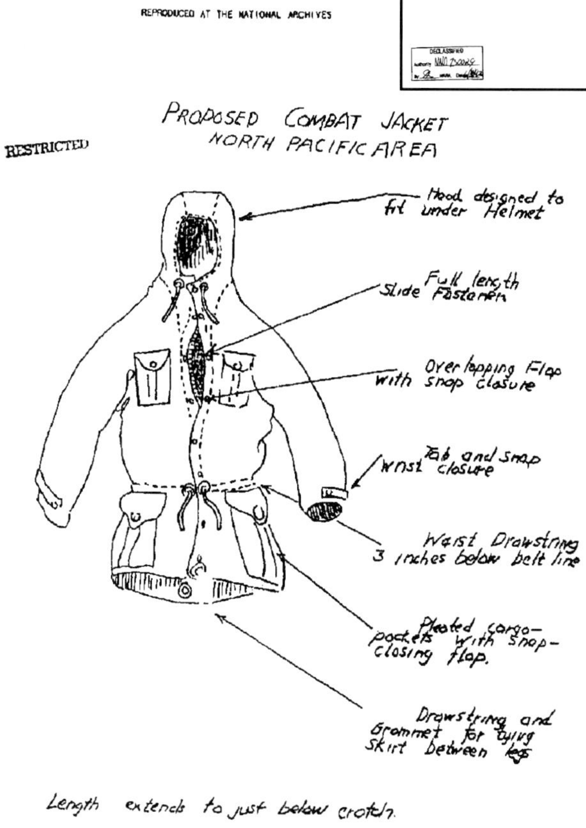

RESTRICTED

PROPOSED COMBAT TROUSERS
for North Pacific Area

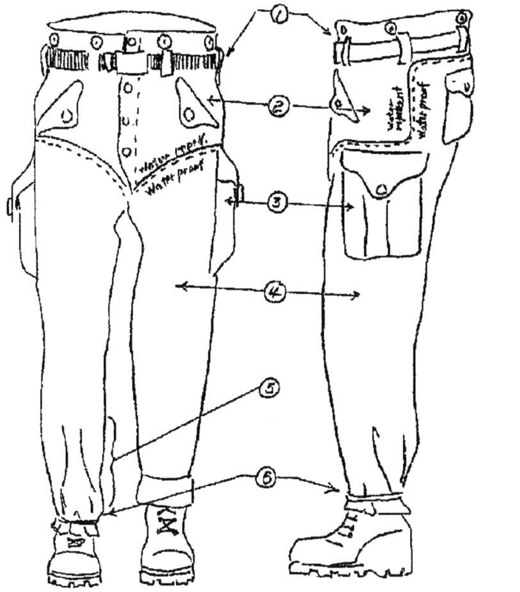

① Belt Loops below suspender buttons. ② Water Repellant material. ③ Pleated Cargo Pockets ④ Waterproof material. ⑤ Zone of greatest wear (Should be reenforced) ⑥ Thong or Tape sewed to back of trouser leg, used for closure around ankle.

All pockets with snap closing flaps.

RESTRICTED

sketches by C. Bradley
working with
Jim Ford

Adak 1944-45

carelessly, fording streams with water almost to the waist. We stood guard in the rain and slept on the tundra in the rain. The fabric made a tough wind breaker and shed the snow quite well. Perspiration was hardly a problem.

After a week or two we had a powwow with Jim, suggesting changes in design of the clothing. I put the main suggestions in the form of a few sketches and left them with Jim. There was no question Jo-cloth was an amazing fabric. Everyone wanted it. Before Jim left for D.C., however, there were signs that in the wear and tear of outdoor living on Adak and the incessant wetting and drying, Jo-cloth was beginning to lose some of its waterproofness. That dampened the spirit a bit, but we already knew from experience that even the Navy's rubberized foul-weather gear and our waterproof mountain tents and tarps suffered from age. Jim said that Research and Development was working on a waterproofing fluid that could be applied to extend the useful life of aging waterproofed cloth. So Jo-cloth looked to be an easy winner if there was enough to go around.

It was early May when Jim Ford returned with the promised boodle. Everyone on the teaching staff blossomed out in Jo-cloth uniforms and broad grins. All the design suggestions we had agreed upon were in place. I suppose we also tested a few of the 100 percent waterproof uniforms but I have no memory or record of it. We were wearing quite a bit the best Aleutian costumes that had yet been made. We now turned our attention from survival and mobility to the art of Aleutian combat.

Jim Ford dressed in new Aleutian uniform made of Jo-cloth

Charles Bradley

Dawn on Mt. Moffet

Winter

On the first of December we held a graduation ceremony for our first class. Here are the results:

16 graduated (suitable to act as guides or instructors)
20 satisfactory (good mountain soldiers)
5 failed
9 departed (left before completion)

This was not a very satisfactory showing, in part because the instructional team and program was not yet in gear and because the candidates were not well selected by their outfits. Physical and mental capacities were not up to the job.

We now had two weeks to shape up for Class 2. There was one upbeat achievement. Candidate S.Sgt. Henry Printup graduated with honors and was invited to join the teaching staff. In January he was given a field commission and became Second Lieutenant Printup, instructor for NPCS. For some reason he was called "Mo." I particularly enjoyed his company because in my free time I was developing a geological notebook and he became interested. Whenever I went prowling I could usually count on Mo's companionship. Also we both enjoyed group singing. So did most of the candidates from Class 2.

During December, Jim Ford was still with us as we went through the period when autumn gave way to winter and the weather shifted subtly from heavy rains spiced with snow to tremendous, often wet, snowstorms. Still more subtly the temperature dropped from slightly above freezing to slightly below. Fog and wind changed not at all.

In a remarkably short time the rough topography of the island was gentled and smoothed as snow drifted into the hollows and avalanched into the gorges. Many a Quonset hut disappeared from the landscape. Those that were occupied could be located by a white stairwell leading down to the door and a black smoking stovepipe protruding from the snow. Unoccupied Quonsets could be located with an avalanche probe.

Somehow in the perpetual gray of blowing rain, snow and fog, a person's spirits and sense of color becomes dulled. But there are such things as perfect winter days on Adak. Stepping out of the tent into my first such day, I was stunned by the degree to which the Aleutian gods had altered the scenery since my last clear look. Crystalline white volcanic cones now rose from the sparkling Pacific and soared into the blue, blue sky. From their summits flew gossamer pennants, woven of snow,

More ski recreation

cloud or volcanic vapors that streamed downwind. It was a fresh new world.

You could hear cheers, shouts and yodeling coming from the tents. Breakfast was given minimal attention. Toni Matt had been out on his skis before sunup. We watched him come down a mountain face a couple of miles away, carving rhythmic curves on the untracked snow. More cheers, yodels and furious action to get on the boards and into the hills. Never was there such an attractive landscape for pent-up downhill skiers.

Most of the instructional staff were reasonably good skiers. A few were experts. I was fairly typical of Midwest skiers of that day. We had grown up on ski jumping and cross-county racing where hills were scarce and mountains nonexistent. Sheer speed and taking the air were not problems, but making turns on a steep slope required special training. Of the small group I brought with me to NPCS from the 10th Mountain Division I was probably the least skilled in downhill skiing. On the other hand, most of the skiing done by a mountain soldier consists of moving across country with a heavy pack. That I could do well enough. But the vista of this day cried "Downhill!"—and I was as eager to try as anyone. How could you lose? Look at Toni Matt!

Yes, look at Toni Matt. Precision at its most beautiful. I hadn't trudged very far toward the crystal mountains before I began to feel misgivings. Ahead, well up on the slope, some of the eager ones were ready to try a test run while I was suspecting that my downhill was going to be all too similar to my up hill—traverse and kick-turn. Why we didn't get a lot of wrenched ankles and knees that morning, I don't know. Three or four were able to make turns and keep going but none looked very much like Toni Matt except Toni Matt. Most who tried took frequent "egg beaters" or cut an irregular path of "linked shell holes." It was hard to believe that the snow cover was not what it appeared to be. It was hard to absorb the disappointment after having watched Toni. Actually it was perhaps the perfect day to learn the truth about the Aleutian snow pack, which after all is the product of Aleutian weather. In brief: cold snow, warm snow; wet snow, dry snow; wind scoured, wind deposited, sheltered powder; old snow, new snow; snow that comes down in crystal plates, fine needles, pellets, or big globs; wind crust, rain crust, no crust, glare ice; good base, collapsing base, no base. Any or most of these snow conditions can show up on one mountain slope in one day on Adak. It makes ski touring with a heavy pack difficult. A downhill run on such a slope is loaded with surprises unless you are a Toni Matt who has seen it all many

Morning patrol; Mt. Moffet in the background

times, can read the pack rapidly and respond instantly with a suitable technique for each condition as it shows up. The closest equivalent I can think of is riding a bucking bronco. There are a few people who do that gracefully, too.

On the bright side, perhaps it was lucky that our mission was to train soldiers to cope with Aleutian conditions as they are. If, instead, we had been charged with developing a large winter recreation area, that could have been discouraging. So out onto the snow, everyone, and start learning!

There is a persistent romantic image of the mountain soldier, and since I can't shake it myself, I have no desire to undermine it or destroy it. There he is, working his way up the impossible cliff, while the enemy looks in the wrong direction. There he

Instruction in the use of crampons and ice axe

goes, dressed in white, skiing ghostlike through the forest, or, invisible on the mountain side, he moves to a position directly above the unsuspecting enemy and cuts loose an avalanche. Less likely images visualize him schussing a steep slope, spraying the enemy with a machine gun, or better still, dropping bombs as he sails across the sky in a record-breaking ski jump.

Forget the fanciful. The reality for the mountain soldier of that day was tough enough. Even the candidates who came to us with a background of many years of civilian downhill skiing had difficulty trying to shake the image of a ski lift, and learn

Adak's latest fad, "uphill skiing." (Helicopters were no help. There weren't any.)

Under any circumstances, the arrival of snow was bound to complicate both the mobility and the training program. Our first snowstorm was a lesson to remember. It arrived during the night when we were about as far as we could get from base camp with its store of snowshoes and skis. Whatever the rest of our excursion was supposed to do, the major canceled it and we took the shortest route toward base. A couple of mountain ranges were part of that route. As usual, we had luck on our side. By Aleutian standards we had received a flurry—about a foot deep. No more snow fell as we slogged our way out. It could just as well have been five feet deep.

Up to the time of heavy snowstorms, the main problem with our mountain tents was their age, which allowed penetration of wind-driven rain. Now a design problem was added. The roof of the mountain tent was not steep enough to do a good job of shedding this brand of snow and there was no overhanging wall at the base to allow some snow accumulation without encroachment on the tent. The result was that if you didn't want the tent to cave in on you, the only solution was to get out of your snug bag, get dressed, go out, and shovel the snow off the tent—and in a couple of hours do it again—and again, and again... I recall one occasion when we had to hole up for a three-day storm. Those were three busy days.

One alternative to mountain tents in snow is to hole up in snow caves of your own making. That works well enough if you have a suitable site, good shovels, and considerable time for construction. Oh yes, if you do use this alternative, be sure to take the shovel with you into the cave.

Our equipment for winter training was simple enough. Boots, snowshoes, skis with climbers, crampons and ice ax, and the Weasel were all we had. Adak snow in midwinter is often so wind packed as to be negotiable by a man on foot. But with the threat of getting caught off base in a heavy snowstorm, snowshoes or skis became absolutely essential for troop mobility.

Snowshoeing is easily learned. Put them on and walk spraddle legged so that they don't interfere with each other. The chief limit to snowshoes comes on slopes so steep that traversing is a must. The webs are too wide to cut a usable ledge. To counter this somewhat, snowshoes are light and easily carried over the traverse if the snow is suitable for walking. But the ability to traverse slopes is so important that snowshoes are uncomfortably limited in mountainous areas.

Skis are the best alternative yet invented for winter foot travel on snowy mountains. The narrow steel-edged boards are ideal on a traverse. With climbers or suitable wax, skiing uphill is often easier than walking. Skis make good use of gravity in descent and speed can be controlled by turns. However, skis have some serious drawbacks in other ways—especially for a soldier. First, it takes years to train a competent ski mountaineer starting from scratch. (Our time limit on Adak was two and a half months). Second, except for flat land operations, a skier is much more limited than a snowshoer in the load he can carry. Picture a soldier with his normal combat load of, say, seventy pounds. He is in his normal downhill position as he descends a slope. His knees are bent. In this way he will be doing the equivalent of many deep knee bends—with seventy pounds on his back. Then there is the matter of the inertia of mass in motion. During the training days in the 10th Mountain Division, I watched

Skijoring behind Weasel

a friend of mine, a good skier from New Hampshire, coming down a gentle slope with perhaps fifty pounds on his back. As he went over a small hump his knapsack lifted him off the ground, turned him upside down and drove him head first into the snowpack, with only his legs and skis visible, waving in the air. Yes, of course there are the Toni Matts who can ski the slopes with heavy loads, but don't count on too many of them.

The ordinary infantry soldier can usually expect some vehicular assistance in personnel and load transportation. Today the helicopter would surely play a major role in mountain operations. For us on Adak in 1944 the Weasel was our only possibility. In the foothill areas of Adak the Weasel was well adapted to winter operation. The many steep-sided gorges that blocked it in summer were completely filled with snow in winter. The

Weasel could not only carry knapsacks and men but could tow a whole squad of men on skis. Much like the snowshoes, however, the wide tracks of the Weasel found their limit on the side hill. Even a mild traverse was enough to derail the tracks. A couple of good mechanics might have the tracks on again in an hour but that was as far as that Weasel was going in that direction. I never saw a Weasel roll over during a traverse but sometimes, as I watched the downhill track digging itself in, I worried a lot about a roll. It was a relief when it derailed itself instead.

With this view of our current strengths and weaknesses, the picture of a possible unit of the Kuril Task Force began to develop in my mind. Logic suggested that:

1. Most of the first graduates would now join NPCS and assist with at least the basic mountain training of the next class.
2. Ski mountaineering training would be confined to those who were excellent skiers to begin with. In combat they would be the highly mobile advance units, the forward intelligence, the scouts of the high ground, the harriers and message carriers. They would have minimum loads so as to be able to cover ground swiftly.
3. The rest, on foot or snowshoes, possibly skis, but otherwise well trained for mountain operations, would make up the main body that moved supplies, weapons and ammunition forward to the combat zone.
4. The Weasels with drivers would assist us all to get as far into the mountains as possible. At that point they would develop a supply dump and help evacuate the injured.

Logic, good or bad, once formulated, tends to anticipate action. My picture of the future began to fade when the first class graduated and all but one immediately disappeared into the fog from whence they came. We had already lost two of our very best mountaineers, Har Quick and George Gagnon. NPCS now numbered fourteen instead of fifteen—hardly a gain in man power. The picture faded even more when there was no essential change in our instructional program. For instance we did not separate the skiers from the nonskiers early on in order to speed up and enhance the special training for each. Were we starting all over?

It was not the first time on this mission that I was beset by a sense of being in the thick of a feverishly active mystery leading—where?

Major Forrest's Litter

Mountain evacuation of an injured person is a chore that anyone has a right to dread—either as evacuator or as victim. I've had two such experiences in my life, including the one recounted earlier. It would be quite okay with me if it never happened again. A civilian on a backpack trip in the mountains usually limits the size of his first-aid kit. For instance, it probably does not include a litter. Instead he would put a lot of faith in his ability to stay out of trouble. Mountain combat changes that rosy picture. You have to assume catastrophe, perhaps a lot of it.

Even without combat, we in NPCS were experiencing an increase in injuries as winter came on. Most were related to skiing, sprained ankles and knees. Most were not serious especially as long as they happened close to base. The standard

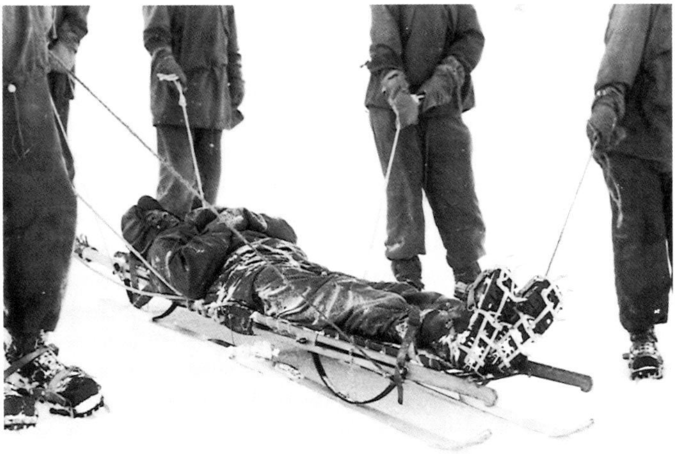

Major Forrest's portable litter/ packboard for all seasons

Major Forrest's litter in action

Major Forrest's litter as two pack boards

military litter of that day was a very durable piece of equipment but in the mountains was a cumbersome nightmare. Well before winter, Major Forrest's inventive mind went to work on the problem. His solution deserves special mention here. In fact a medal would not have been exorbitant. At one stroke his litter helped solve several severe evacuation problems.

Unassembled, the Forrest Litter was two packboards on which two men could lash their normal loads. Any two packboards could be locked together to become a litter, light but durable enough to carry a heavy man. (We tested it with more sand bags than we could lift.) On the ground it rested on four strap-iron, rocker-like runners. Thus it could be carried like a standard litter or could be dragged over firm snow and even tundra if the hummocks were not too large. Finally, the runners were easily bolted to a pair of skis, creating a very serviceable sled. With some guide ropes and a little practice three skiers could maneuver the loaded sled rapidly and safely down the slopes. By lashing the injured person tightly to the litter, we were able to belay him down a vertical cliff. Here the strap-iron runners functioned to prevent hang-ups on the irregularities of the rock face. (The stump-like legs of the standard litter were prone to hang-ups.)

It is safe to say that the major's litter did much to cheer the men, especially the medics who had had enough experience to dread evacuations. Jim Ford was very interested in this litter and featured it in his report to OQMG. At that time they had developed light tough plywood packboards that Jim thought could be readily adapted to the litter assignment. If so, there might be a chance that their fabrication would be in time for Forrest Litters to become part of the first-aid kit for the Kuril Task Force. It was an exciting idea. I wonder whatever became of it.

Winter Morale

"It has come to the attention of this headquarters that Company C has low morale. This situation will be corrected immediately." (Unforgettable orders issued by Major [?], First Battalion at Camp Grant, Illinois, August 1941.)

It's the long dark subarctic winter night. When the lamps are doused and the diversion of chatter ends, the ache of loneliness sneaks up on a soldier who has not been home for a long time. Many in NPCS had not seen home since Pearl Harbor Day three years before. Since marrying Maynie two years ago, I had seen her briefly, perhaps a dozen times, and my son, now a year old, twice very briefly. Many in NPCS had not been that lucky. Sometimes I would look at the men and wonder how they were doing. Clearly they were fine during the day. There was a lot of banter and horseplay or serious attention on mountaineering instruction. But what of the night? It's not an easy subject to probe.

The blinds went up for me one evening when I was in the midst of my usual chore, censoring the mail. Normally I would look for key words and phrases that might give comfort to Tokyo Rose, but all of a sudden I was reading a nightmare of domestic life gone haywire, of loneliness and desperation. The soldier whose letter I was reading I knew only casually. He was not one of the instructional team. He had come off a Midwest farm, was a hard worker, generally quiet and private, but he smiled easily in conversation. From his letter I judged he was married and his wife was running the farm in his absence—now two years long.

Her last letter must have been a bomb out of the blue. Apparently with no early warning, she told him that she was pregnant and wanted a divorce so she could marry the father and have a legitimate child. The new man had been giving her a much needed hand on the farm and she, overworked, lonely, and depressed, had given herself in return.

My guess is that she had remained silent, hoping that her husband might return soon and that life might get shaken into place again. With the unwanted pregnancy there was no way to cushion the blow. It was devastating. In an avalanche of words he tried to dissuade her from the divorce. He tried to tell her how much he loved her, that he could understand her loneliness, didn't blame her for what she did, that he would love and cherish the child as his own, but that he needed her, needed her, needed her. "Please, please be there when I come home!"

Blotches on the ink writing confirmed the depth of his desperation. By the time I'd gotten that far I couldn't be sure some of the blotches weren't mine. That young man was speaking for many of us. When I met him the next morning, I smiled and asked him how things were going. He smiled back and said, "Fine. What's on for today?"

Perhaps in a later day our more casual view of marriage would make such news less devastating, but at that time and place it wasn't easy to forget this letter and the reminder that home, though heaven, was far, far away and not entirely under our control. Ultimately when it was clear that the war was beginning to move in our favor I unloaded this story in a letter to Maynie. It ended, "I want you to know that I love you and am as fully dependent on you as that man was on his wife. If I got home and found you with a kid that wasn't mine I would understand and want to adopt him to keep us together."

Maynie's reply in her next letter brought the earth back under my feet again. "Well, for goodness sake, why didn't you tell me that earlier?"

One feature of our second mountaineering class stands out in my memory. Most of its officers and many of its enlisted men enjoyed group singing. They infected NPCS, especially me.

I had grown up around a piano with my six brothers and a father who knew many songs and the parts thereto. He taught us the parts by ear, one at a time, until we had a fairly respectable family chorus. At family gatherings and on camping trips

The singing group of our second class

there was always a lot of singing, and some of it was even good. Father referred to us as the Campfire Quartet. Ever since, group singing has been one of my perpetual hungers. I had to discover that good group singing just for the fun of it is not one of the great American traditions. When it does show up, that is a time of treasure to be cherished.

The first night I heard vocal harmony oozing out of one of the tents, I was instantly magnetized, walked over to the tent, barged in to listen, then hum, and then add voice. There seemed to be no feeling of territorialism. I was in. We began regular evening gatherings. Over time we learned songs from each other, worked out harmonies and parts. You could feel the lift of spirit when a choice bit of harmony came through okay. Pretty soon some of the members were creating new words for old tunes. Finally one evening one of the officers arrived with an original melody. We all pitched in to learn it and help weave the harmony to round it out. We were growing in size. Bonds were developing and yet there was no director or leader as such. The gang was evolving like an organism and was even functioning something like one.

Some of the enlisted men came out with "Bitchin' Songs" that surely must have helped defuse their frustrations and exasperations. The songs were such as to invite a rash of additional verses until they were almost ballads. Sometimes the tents would rock with laughter. In answer to an unspoken question, yes, there were songs that featured ugliness, filth and depravity, but most of these died early and quietly of their own sickness. In any case they seemed not to lend themselves to the specialty of the house, multipart harmony. I can recall one bawdy song that got started and survived primarily because it generated so many hilarious verses from so many different people. Group laughter has its own therapeutic value.

Jim Cavanah, one of our noncoms, was a Blackfoot from Montana. His Irish surname dated back to the building of the North Pacific railroad. Whether it was the Irish or the Blackfoot in him he occasionally joined in the singing and even introduced us to some of the tribal chants. I can still dredge up a short Indian love song Jim taught me, and I taught my guitar. The words are those of a young buck singing to his wife. Translated and omitting the introductory wails and terminal "omph!" he says, "I would love you very much if you would only stop beating me." Sounds reasonable.

It may be significant that no one in the gang expressed any desire to present concerts at the little local theater even though we were probably good enough and would have been welcome since local talent was sparse on Adak. But no. The singing of our group seemed to be a homemade product for home consumption only, more like a Sunday softball game.

I can understand how singing can grow in an outfit, but how does it get started? In the early days of the 10th Mountain Division on Mt. Rainier, almost overnight we had a glee club. Was it the prevailing Swiss/Austrian influence that linked snow, skis, and song? On invitation the group did give a couple of concerts in Seattle. Our finest hour, however, came one evening at Paradise Lodge on Mt. Rainier when a bunch of us sent a night letter to a friend in the Midwest who was getting married. It consisted of some new words to an old Austrian ski song. The telephone operator at Longmire listened carefully to the words. After she had reread them to us we thanked her and hung up. In a couple of minutes she called back. "Before I send this on I was wondering if you would sing the song for me?" I shoehorned the bunch into the phone booth and we gave our four-part best. She thanked us and hung up. A couple of minutes later she called again. "I was passing the message on to the Seattle operator. She's on the line now and wonders if you would sing the song for her too?" We would.

In many countries music is an integral part of the military. It may be the binding force of men's voices in harmony rather than the lone voice of the captain that holds the company together as it moves toward the attack. Some of the hair-lifting songs of the Don Cossacks would be quite sufficient to gelatinize an enemy listening to their approach.

For me, however, the singing on Adak was medicine, pure and simple. It broke up the long, dark night syndrome. Instead of dreading lights out I slipped off to sleep thinking of more tunes and better harmonies. Tomorrow there would be another fest.

Ahvakana

It would be a mistake not to give special mention of Ahvakana in this story. He, more than anyone else, was responsible for the morale of NPCS since among his many chores was that of mail orderly.

His full name was Lloyd Ahvakana, but "Lloyd" is mundane. "Ahvakana" is musical and mysterious so that's what he was always called. He joined us at Dutch Harbor and, long before he became mail orderly, he was one of the best liked men in the outfit. He always had a smile on his face with a bright laugh just behind ready to jump out. An Eskimo from Point Barrow, he was short, lithe, had straight black hair, was handsome, and smart as a new whip. With this built-in sunny, friendly disposition, it is not surprising that, even excluding the mail, Ahvakana was a general morale booster.

Sometimes in our concern for ourselves we take the Ahvakanas for granted. Even a mail orderly needs mail once in a while, especially in winter. At Point Barrow in those days, winter mail moved in and out by dog sled which often took weeks. The men began to notice fewer smiles and laughs. A general quietness had settled down on Ahvakana. One bright guy guessed the situation and glimpsed a possible solution. He wrote to his own parents in Minnesota, explaining the whole situation about Ahvakana. Being big hearted, action minded Americans, they passed the story, including Ahvakana's Adak address, to the local newspaper.

Within a week Ahvakana got his first mail in months. To be exact there were 81 letters. That was just the beginning. Next day he got over 100 and the third day over 200 plus several packages. In a short time he was getting over half the mail for NPCS. I doubt if anything like that had ever happened before in the Aleutians.

After his first shock, Ahvakana's smile returned and then his laugh. With his usual generosity he passed the letters around to everyone. You could hear the cheers emanating from the Quonset huts all over. The morale on all of Adak went up.

Ahvakana got many nice gifts. He also received a few offers of marriage. It was typical of this young man that he acknowledged all the letters and gifts. There were a select few he answered individually. For the main body he typed out a mimeograph letter that might, to some recipients, have been a treasure. I treasure the copy he gave me, and I copy it here to complete the story.

Dear Friend:

I hope that you will forgive me for this mimeographed reply to your most welcomed letter, but I received more letters than it is possible for me to answer each one individually. I appreciate your writing to me very much and wish that I had the time to write a letter to each person that was kind enough to write to me, but 100 letters a day is entirely too many to answer personally. My duties here at the school keep me very busy; along with my mail orderly duties I do messenger work for the headquarters' staff. My duties, however, are not too strenuous as I have a jeep of my own to use when delivering and picking up messages.

I have been in the army since December 1941 and have spent all of my life, both as a civilian and as a soldier in Alaska and the Aleutian Islands. My home is Point Barrow, Alaska; it is the northernmost part of the North American continent. I'm 23 years old and lived there until I entered the army. My home town is a small town of about 600 persons, mostly my own people, the Eskimo. My parents still live there and are enjoying good health. When the war is over I do not know whether I will return there or not. At present I am not married and my plans seem to be like the other soldiers; that is, "Wait until it is all over and see what will result."

Up to the time I was twelve years old the only language I could speak was Eskimo. At that time I started learning English, and speak it quite fluently now. As in different countries, my language varies with the different localities. My particular dialect is spoken from Point Barrow to a small village, up the coast, named Kotzebue. Although the distance is only 350 miles, natives from these two areas cannot understand the language spoken by surrounding tribes. This may seem quite strange to you, but I understand that states the size of Illinois, and others experience almost the same differentiation. The isolation here makes the great difference.

Travel to and from Point Barrow is very much limited. In the summertime it is done by airplane and ship, and in the wintertime by dog sled.

In the winter mail is brought only three times to my home. Letters are relayed from Kotzebue to Point Hope, and from there to Point Barrow. Outgoing mail is carried by the driver to Point Hope and is exchanged with the driver from Kotzebue so that he can return to Point Barrow with the incoming mail. From Kotzebue to Nome it is carried by dog sled or airplane, depending on the weather.

My people at home make their living by hunting and trapping. A few of the natives are employed by Government employees as janitors, as they are doing their best to help the natives. There are more facts about my home that I would like to tell you about, but they are under the title of military secrets now. We will all know more about my home after the war is over.

Thanking you again for your kind remembrances, I remain

Sincerely yours,
Lloyd Ahvakana

Enter the Photographer

One February day, when slush squalls were plastering both Shagak Camp and the candidates of Class 2, the mail Weasel arrived with a visitor who was destined to bring variety into our lives. He was a noncom wearing the insignia of the Signal Corps. In fact he was a photographer for the army magazine *Yank* and was assigned to us for a week to do a photo story of NPCS.

To this new aberration I had two instant but unrelated visceral responses. First was the pleasant thought of a little shop talk. I had been a commercial photographer when the army interrupted my life in July 1941. There was a brief period of transition when I tried to convince Selective Service to select me for the photo mapping service. Too bad. They were not taking men over twenty-eight years old. I was thirty. That was a long time ago and under the pressure of war, photography was evolving at the speed of light—doing some amazing things. It would be great to sit down with this army photographer and catch up.

My second instant response was shock. NPCS was supposed to be top secret. A photo splash in *Yank* would be on Tokyo Rose's desk while the ink was still wet. This invasion of military privacy could be no run-of-the-mill goof. But I kept my thoughts to myself.

Our visitor was all bundled up in a fur-lined parka, trousers, and mukluks, all set for the North Pole. The eight-mile ride in the open Weasel from Adak Base had pretty well soaked him through. He was well chilled. Today we would say that he had shelter readiness. We helped him unload his chest of photographic material, found an empty bunk with the other noncoms, and dug up some clothing better suited to the Aleutians.

The more we helped him, the more concerned we became. Did he have a change of underwear while his current garb was drying? "No, but no problem. I'll be OK." Did he have any over snow equipment? "What's that?" Well, things like snowshoes and skis. "No, but I'll be OK." How did he expect to get around for pictures? "No problem. I'll just ride in the Weasel and take pictures from it."

Obviously, we were dealing with a gap that was going to be difficult to bridge. We explained that the Weasel had done all it could to get him to Shagak Camp. From here on to the training area was exclusively foot soldier territory. He stopped saying "No problem" and asked, "Well, how do I get there?" We suggested snowshoes, found a spare pair of bear paws—small snowshoes, shorter and rounder than the usual trail models—and some boots to fit, showed him how to attach the bear paws and told him that when he was dry and thawed out, go out, get the bear paws on and walk around locally until he got the hang of it. "Then we'll take you to where the action is. By the way, do you have a knapsack or some device to carry your camera and emergency gear?" "Well, no."

So we scrounged a rucksack and suggested that after he had mastered walking, he should load up the sack and walk around with that for a while. "By the way, you don't have a compass, do you?" "No." So our last suggestion was that while we were gone he should stay close enough to camp to see the tents. In storms like this it was easy to get lost and never be found.

As we left for the class, it was clear from the sober look on his face that he had been impressed by our conversation. The major and I dropped by the cook's tent and asked that he take a look out the flap once in a while to note the progress of our photographer.

In late afternoon, when we all closed in on camp, there was no sign of the photographer—until we entered the tent. He was lying on his cot reading a magazine. We introduced him to his tent mates and asked him how the snowshoeing went. "Well," he said, "I decided to just rest up today and go after it tomorrow." The cook later confirmed our suspicion. "He never came out of the tent." I looked at the major. He shrugged. "No problem," he said.

When we returned from the hills the next afternoon, the photographer was on his cot reading a magazine. When asked how it went he said, "OK, I guess. I walked around until I got bored and came in." The cook's observations contained more details. Yes, he did walk around some, but a great deal of the time his head was in the snow and his feet in the air from tripping the toes or from one snowshoe stepping on the other.

This was getting serious. We were in the thick of a relatively difficult and dangerous instruction period with the candidates. Rock climbing in stormy weather takes a lot of attention to avoid unnecessary danger and catastrophe. Even if, as with Mohammed, the mountain came to the photographer, there would be no way to move him safely up into good picture-taking positions.

On the third day our photographer was ready to give up. At least he understood why mobility was an important part of our curriculum. He looked humbled and sad as we chatted. Then a bright thought shot through my mind. "Why don't you loan me that Speed Graphic of yours? It's a camera I used for years. I'll

Sergeant Toni Matt makes Yank *cover*

shoot a batch of pictures and if we are lucky there may be something that will keep you from going back empty handed."

Gone was that sad sack look. "No kidding! Could you do that? I've got trays, developer, fixer, the works right here in the chest. I could develop the negatives at night. Then we'll know whether we have something or not. If necessary we could make a second try before my time is up."

And so it was. After two days of shooting he had some negatives and I had the fun of being a photographer on an assignment again, plus the pleasure of a little shop talk on the side. He certainly was no mountain man, but I did enjoy his company and wished him luck as he pulled out in the Weasel.

If I could have looked ahead a half year to the day when *Yank* finally published my photography I would certainly not have worried about it falling into the hands of Tokyo Rose. There was no photo story, just one picture, but that was the cover of *Yank Weekly*, August 31, 1945. They had selected my favorite negative. The major, Toni Matt and I had a great time setting it up. It portrayed Toni belayed on the face of a cliff. Cradled in his arms was a light machine gun and a belt of ammunition. Toni looked very businesslike and threatening, but in truth, the major, the magazine and I had succumbed to the inevitable romantic image of the mountain soldier, rather than anything approximating combat. It was great! Tokyo Rose could well have fallen in love with Toni.

Incidentally, the Signal Corps took the credit for the photo, but I had the fun.

Mike

MIKE AND THE COMEDIANS

First, you must meet Mike. We were "doing" mobility far from base in the jumble of hills on the south side of Adak, when out of the fog loped a large wolf moving to the attack—at least that was my first impression. Instead it was an Alaskan husky that thought he had spotted friends, and he was correct. A more handsome creature never lived. He weighed perhaps ninety pounds, was long legged, and had paws about the size of my hand. When he put those paws on my shoulder, as he liked to do, we were eye to eye.

One of the gang called him Mike. He accepted the name without question, joined the group and was with us until NPCS was disbanded. We never did find out what he was doing so far from any human settlement. He seemed well fed, in perfect shape, but no one back at base had ever seen him. He was immune to the weather but on a tough night was often invited into some mountain tent to help keep the place warm.

Mike reminded me a little of Jack London's fictional dog "Buck." He was very silent, never barked; he hardly even growled. Sometimes he would make deep soft musical sounds when the boys wrestled with him.

Back at Adak Base there were scads of dogs, all sizes, shapes, and colors. But as Bob Niss said, "There is something in their eyes and faces that suggest they are all related." The day when Mike marched into town with our gang, it was hate at first sight. You could tell where Mike was by the yelping and snarling, but he strolled around town as though the other dogs weren't there. And they, on their part, were pretty cautious about doing more than yelp. One day, however, a small group ganged up and attacked Mike. Silent and seemingly detached, he stood and watched them come. In about a minute one dog was dying, two were crippled, and the rest had left the field. The message must have gotten around because he was never attacked again, and the yelpers did their yelping from a safe distance.

Despite all Mike's calm, quiet power the day came when he encountered an enemy he could not conquer, control, or shake, and we were there to see his ignominy several times. He was trotting along with the gang in the field when a flight of four ravens came skimming over the tundra and took up positions in flight about three feet above Mike's head. They proceeded to make quite insulting remarks within Mike's hearing. Mike paid no attention to this trash. He just looked forward and kept trotting. The ravens kept hovering and talking. Once in a while one would dip down, almost touch Mike's head and then swoop quickly up again. This went on for many minutes with no observable change. But beneath Mike's poker face he must have been storing up a load of dynamite. All of a sudden he exploded his own length up into the air, yelling and snapping with rage. The ravens knew their game well. With great precision they rose just enough to stay clear of the airborne teeth and paws, then settled down over Mike's head again. The game started over. After a half hour of this play and many wonderful but unsuccessful leaps, Mike was badly in need of a psychiatrist, and the ravens, bored, drifted off. They would return another day. In fact they clearly enjoyed the days when Mike was available for play. I hope that there came the day when Mike nailed his raven in full flight and reestablished his self-esteem and imperturbability.

Adak town in winter was about as busy as in any other time of year, but when, as happened a few times in the winter of 1944–45, a flock of ravens gathered on the network of power lines near the generating plant, mundane chores were abandoned. The town of Adak leaned back against the ice-encrusted Quonsets, watched, applauded and tossed tasty tidbits at the performers. The ravens on their part responded with a high-wire circus which included their own cheerful running comments. Unlike their shy behavior in summer, they showed no uneasiness at the size and proximity of the human mob. Rather, they seemed to enjoy this attention and appreciation for their acrobatic prowess. Here is a representative list of stunts as I remember them.

A raven flying in would make an upright landing on a horizontal wire and promptly fall forward or backward without letting go. Hanging upside down by his feet, he would swing back and forth, increasing his arc with each swing until he was standing upright once more.

Sometimes a second raven would join him. Immediately they would try to dislodge each other, upside down, right-side up, batting each other with wings, beaks, doing anything but letting go of the wire.

Once only I saw a raven land on the wire and execute a giant swing, ending upright again.

One raven hanging upside down walked back and forth on the wire in that position. Then suddenly he let go with one foot. Hanging by the other he flapped his wings and pivoted around part way and back again, squawking and putting on a great fuss. It looked as though he had gotten his foot caught in a trap and was trying to thrash free. He finally let go altogether and flew away.

There was one stunt that was a favorite, both with our gang and the big black birds. A raven would land high on one of the sloping guy wires and slide down sideways at fairly high speed. Before hitting ground or the anchor stake, he spread his wings and transferred to the air. Several times we saw two or three en route down the cable at a time.

This ends my recitation of *Corvid* antics. I doubt if there is anything new to science here and there may even be a few aberrations of observation and memory. "Raven play behavior," as it is called in the literature, was brand new to me at that time and utterly fascinating. Since then I have watched the same species in the Northern Rockies of the lower forty-eight but my strong impression is that the Aleutian arm of the family is far more inventive, more daring, more comic, even more enthusiastic. Bob Niss said, "Aw, they're just plain crazy. It's to be expected if you stay in the Aleutians very long." Later I actually found some confirmation for Bob's human implications. It was at a tiny outpost far from Adak town.

On the first of March we celebrated the end of our second class of fifty candidates, ten officers, and forty enlisted men. There were thirteen graduates (instructor types), nine who were rated satisfactory as mountain men, eight failed, and twenty who departed without finishing.

The figures tend to belie the feeling we had that this class was significantly better than the first. For one thing, the weather presented many more problems and problems of greater severity. One factor, skiing with heavy packs, was extremely tough. We had to put quite a few of the candidates on snowshoes, which tended to separate them from the skiers, which in turn complicated the curriculum. They were a hard-working cheerful gang and pleasant to have around. I especially missed the singing when they left. Probably to cheer us up, on May 2 all the commissioned officers of NPCS took one step up in rank. It was now Lieutenant Colonel Forrest, Major Krause, Captain Hitchcock, and Captain Bradley. That was a bit scary because it implied that I was qualified to lead a company (approximately 100 men) into battle. Considering my past activities and training, that seemed a bit premature. But there it was.

On the 15th of March when the third class arrived, there were some unexplained shifts in the norm. Instead of fifty candidates we had fifty-three, and instead of two and a half months, we had only two months. Finally, this class incorporated three very different groups: thirteen officers and twenty-seven enlisted men from the Alaskan Department; two officers and fourteen enlisted men from the Marine Corps; four officers from Strategic Services, Washington, D.C. Now what? This sounded more like a task force mix, including pressure to hurry. Were things heating up? The school staff was bowstring taut as instruction began.

Right from the start it was the marines who set the pace and everyone caught the spirit. I cannot remember if they had had battle experience but they acted that way.

Spring

Spring: when green hummocks of tundra suddenly began to emerge through the snow cover, we woke up to the fact that spring was sneaking in. The storms were less savage. There was less snow in them and more rain. The temperature was spending more time above freezing. Gurgling water was audible beneath the snow pack which by now was visibly sagging over the buried gorges. The collapse of snow tunnels in the gorges and the afternoon slush avalanches on mountain slopes were new hazards to be dealt with in the survival program. (A wet snow avalanche has the nasty habit of solidifying almost instantly after it stops moving. Anyone caught and buried in one has a poor chance of survival.)

While winter 1944–1945 was fading away, I was in tenuous contact with buddies in the 10th Mountain Division who were fighting their way down the Apennines, the backbone of Italy. My purpose was to get their firsthand view of the effectiveness of our mountain training and equipment in combat—especially if they had any suggestions for improvements. My best correspondents were Capt. Gordon Stimson, who had been with our

View of Mt. Moffet from Shagak Bay

detachment to NPCS for two months, and Lt. Ralph Bromaghin, a singing buddy during Mt. Rainier days. They both had analytical minds and took the time to answer my questions and suggest new twists to mountain combat training.

Another reason to keep track of the 10th was that it was becoming increasingly clear that Germany was caving in. When it did, the war in Europe would be over. Our military power, currently tied up in Europe, could turn its attention to Japan. Maybe, just maybe, some of the 10th would be on the Kuril Task Force after all.

Another 10th Mountain friend of mine, John Montagne, also fighting in Italy, understood that the 10th was on the list for early departure back to the states. They would have a hasty home leave and then be reassigned to the Pacific to participate in an attack on the Japanese half of the island, Sakhalin, just west of the Kurils. Was that the target for our task force? By this time I had heard so many variations of our mission that one more was no surprise.

There were some of the 10th who would not be there. I didn't know it at the time, but Bromaghin's last note to me arrived after he was killed in action. The note told of a new weapon that was a must for mountain combat. It was a kind of superlight cannon. One man could carry it and fire it from his shoulder. It had the power to wipe out a tank. Ralph referred to it as a "bazooka."

We at NPCS had a cannon, but to use it in the mountains pushed us to the limit. Originally it had been designed to be carried by a pack mule. There was no such critter in Adak. The nearest thing to a mule was a big powerful stubborn soldier. By breaking the cannon down into five separate loads that could be lashed to five separate packboards it became portable—by five separate but very powerful men who carried nothing else. When mounted, it shot a thirty-seven millimeter projectile and was quite accurate up to two or three miles. At a mile or less, its trajectory was so flat that it could be "bore sighted." When you looked through the barrel, what you saw was what you hit. It was fun to shoot after it was emplaced but—well, we finally dropped it from our armament because of weight limitations. We had several riflemen who were fairly accurate at a mile with the old World War I Springfield thirty-caliber bolt-action rifle with telescopic sight. In terrain like that of Adak where mountains are always obstructing the horizontal view, mortars and howitzers that lobbed their shells high in the air and over the mountains were of more use than the big flat-trajectory cannon. The day of the bazooka and recoilless rifles was just dawning, but too late for NPCS.

Five-man portable cannon. Shagak Bay and bars in background

Toni Matt demonstrating light mortar without tripod or base plate

Cannons were not the only weapons we questioned because of weight. Fortified by the opinions of some of our buddies in Italy, we were becoming doubtful about the most basic infantry weapon of the day—the M-1 rifle. It was a bit heavier than the Springfield and less accurate. Since it was an automatic rifle, there was a tendency to use it as a kind of machine gun to spray the enemy with lead rather than as a precision weapon. Used thus the M-1 was something of an ammunition hog. Ammunition is a heavy item, and more ammunition is even heavier.

A new lighter weight scheme for Aleutian infantry was being discussed: Scale down but retain accuracy. For instance, in each squad one or two of the best shots would carry a Springfield with telescopic sight for accuracy at long distances. The others, including the officers, would carry thirty-caliber automatic carbines. They were considerably lighter than the M-1 and used lighter ammunition. They would be useful for fire power at fairly close range. In terms of heavier weapons, the Browning automatic rifle would replace the light, air-cooled machine gun. The light machine gun would replace the heavy water-cooled machine gun. Light and heavy mortars would remain as assigned.

Without a live enemy on which to test the new Light Battalion concept, the best we could do was to simulate a battle situation. Just southeast of Shagak Camp was a spur off Bitchin' Ridge that we picked for our first battle ground. It was far enough away from camp to prevent stray bombs, shells, bullets and other military garbage from landing on camp, but near enough so that "in the unlikely event" of an injury, evacuation would not be unnecessarily difficult.

The designated enemy was located on a rounded knoll at the far end of the spur. Assuming no fog, it was a marvelous observation post with an unobstructed view of almost 300 degrees including all Adak village and Kuluk Bay. The enemy consisted of a sinister group of three soldiers, looking for all the world like three dark-colored sacks filled with grass and rocks to hold them down in a wind. There was a low wall of rocks to protect them from wind and bullets. As we walked away from this piece of modern art, they looked more and more sinister in the gathering fog until at 200 feet they disappeared.

Now for the attack. We would need a preliminary heavy barrage to soften them up before the foot soldiers became involved. Down at Adak village I talked to another Captain Bradley (a nonrelative) who flew a P-38. The project sounded like fun to him. "First, though," he said, "we should make an exploratory flight to be sure of the target and surrounding terrain. Want to go with me?" You betcha!

When I arrived at the plane, a ground crew was busy taking out a big piece of equipment from behind the pilot's seat. Something wrong? Would we be able to fly? The men actually were removing the radio to make a niche for me. There is no second seat in a P-38. I was about to ride piggyback. "Don't you need that radio to make the flight?" Naw. Not on a day like this. Pile in and see if you can stuff yourself into that cubby. "Don't we wear parachutes?" Naw, if anything went wrong you couldn't get out of that slot fast enough to do any good anyway. I'm not wearing one either. After being shoehorned in, I was something like a bullfrog crowded into a ping-pong ball. My knees were up by my armpits. My feet were almost on the captain's shoulders. My head was bent forward so my chin was pushed into my chest. The captain was right. There was no way I could get out without a corkscrew. And in that condition we headed for the wild blue yonder.

What a beautiful flying ship is a P-38. With the two engines off to the side, there was little of the usual vibration and roar. Just a quiet force lifting us like a feather. "Ever do a roll in an airplane?" the captain asked when we had a little altitude. "No," I wheezed. With no physical sensation at all the horizon ahead of us rotated 360 degrees. I was so pressed in on all sides that I couldn't distinguish the pull of gravity from my compact niche.

We flew over the target area first at high altitude and then quite low, then returned to base. When they helped me out, I was afraid I'd retain the shape of that niche for the rest of my life, but in a couple of days I was almost my military self again. Captain Bradley said, "Whenever you're ready, give me a call. I'll fly over and make two bombing runs at right angles to the spur. That will keep the ridge line clear for the infantry."

One late afternoon at twilight our gang moved up a valley at the base of the spur where, by peeking around a rock shoulder, we could just see the enemy diagonally above us. Sgt. Bill Bowes set up his heavy mortar and took some sights between the streamers of fog. Finally he drove a peg into the ground near the mortar. By readjusting his sight to the peg, the mortar was aimed and the shell calculated to land on the knoll, whether or not the enemy was visible. When it was dark I joined a detachment of infantry quietly working its way up close to the crest where we bivouacked for the night. We had radio contact with the group below and with Captain Bradley at the airport. Tomorrow was D-Day, Jr.

In the predawn darkness we crept toward the enemy, keeping the crest between us and our target. Finally we had them in view. The ridge was just barely above the cloud deck, colored now with the rich tints of dawn. Looking west we could see the

Fuji-like cone of Kanaga floating above the clouds. Our radio man contacted Captain Bradley. He was off and coming. Bill Bowes and the heavy weapons gang down in the fog at the base of the ridge acknowledged and took cover. Soon we could hear the engines but had trouble seeing the plane. It was skittering along barely in and out of the cloud blanket. Suddenly it rose up to pass over the enemy and cut loose the first bomb. We ducked down to avoid any bits of shattered rock. But the bomb, passing very close over the target, sailed clear and landed way down in the valley with a splendid orange flash and a roar that echoed around the hills for many seconds. In due time Captain Bradley approached again and kicked the second bomb loose. This time it fell short and shook us with the blast against the mountain wall below the target. Then he departed with a mixture of cuss words and apologies.

It was Bill Bowes' turn. In the heavy fog and semidarkness of the valley he carefully sighted his 81-mm mortar on the peg and fired. We could hear the whump as the shell started. Up through the fog bank it came, arced over and dropped right on the enemy's rookery, blasting it to pieces. We gave Bill a big cheer but told him it was an accident unless he could do it twice in a row. He did. There wasn't really much that the infantry boys could do to improve things, but we gave the remnants a barrage from our carbines, crept up close, showered them with hand grenades, and called it a day. That night Bill was decorated, roasted, toasted, and showered with a bucket of ice water from the pond.

That short, one-sided war was no thorough test of our new lightweight concept but, at least to the infantry arm that had to make the night climb with heavy loads, it was a step in the right direction. The point seemed to be, "Travel light, close in swiftly, and unless you are backed up by a line of ammunition bearers, don't count on much more than one good solid bash. If you haven't obliterated the enemy, retreat rapidly, and try again later." We never got a chance to find out whether the idea was really sound.

On the 15th of May we celebrated the termination of Class 3, the wildest of all our classes. In keeping with their abnormal routine, a few days before graduation the marines and the strategic service officers suddenly packed up and left—no certificates. That was a letdown. These were the best candidates we would have. I hope the training was of use to them, whatever they were up to. Their swift, unheralded departure increased our feeling that something big and urgent was building out there in the fog.

The forty Alaska candidates left their best record yet and the best of all our classes before and after. Twenty-three attained graduate status, fourteen were satisfactory, and three departed early with the others.

Again we had two weeks' respite before the next class—plenty of time to enjoy late May. Three events took place in that interim. I record them here, one for me and one for you and one for the record.

Chance Meeting

It was a pleasant spring day when our gang took the six-mile hike from Shagak Camp to Adak Base for a weekend in civilization. As we crossed the low pass, I was keeping my eye out for the blooming of our earliest spring flower, the narcissus anemone, and admiring the rare view of Great Sitkin volcano with its vapor plume trailing off to the southeast—toward home. Maybe I was thinking of home, too. The last thing I could have anticipated for this particular time and place was an event that would change the course of the rest of my life.

Coming toward us up the trail from town was a man carrying a knapsack and walking with a brisk springy stride. He was medium sized and looked well adapted to the outdoors. Since it was rare that we ever saw any non-NPCS person on that trail, I stopped to get acquainted. He stuck his hand out and said, "I'm Bob Sharp and I'm looking for the NPCS."

"You're looking at the NPCS marching right by you at this very instant," I said. "What can we do for you?"

"In town they told me you lived out this way, so, well, it was a good day for a hike."

He was on a mission for the 10th Air Corps to examine Adak's emergency foods for downed pilots and had been told that we had done quite a lot with that subject. Here was a chance to save time and effort. I signaled to Bob Niss to go ahead with the group while I stayed behind to help our visitor. To tell the truth, Adak town held no real charm for me. I agreed with Mr. Sharp that this was indeed a good day for a hike, a good day to think of something other than mountain training for those who didn't like mountains very much.

My flower sketch book was in my pack so we went over to a big boulder, sat down and discussed what we had tested as edible plants, roots, and berries. It was the wrong time of year to see much on the ground, but Mr. Sharp seemed to know his plants very well. As far as I was concerned, except for the berries, which were delicious, most of the edible plants required a pretty severe emergency to make them edible.

"How about sea food?" I asked. "You don't even need an emergency for that." So we talked about mussels, the real backbone of sea food opportunity. They were large, tasty and ubiquitous along all the rocky shores. We talked about crabs, shrimp, and salmon (in season). I was a little reluctant to mention the giant clams because our only source, Shagak's tidal flat, was beginning to reveal signs of too many hungry mountain trainees. But I was beginning to like this man. (His name was now "Bob" instead of "Mr.") So I eased into the subject of clams with, "Do you like clams on the half-shell?" I didn't tell him that the half-shells I had in mind were about ten inches long. We finally bridged that gap, too, and I revealed the location of the treasure.

As we got up to continue the hike, he pointed to the lone boulder we had been sitting on. "What do you make of that?"

I answered, "Glacier, I suppose, but I can't decide whether it came off Mt. Moffet to the north or that mountain range to the south."

"Is there evidence of glaciers to the south?"

"Yes, and I think it was separate from the Moffet glacier because there are striations in a couple of high passes to the south that suggest a fairly thick ice sheet over there flowing this way."

"You've had some geology," Bob suggested. I told him I had a bachelor's degree in geology from the University of Wisconsin, Madison. "Do you keep a notebook?" I took my notebook from my shirt pocket. Bob looked it over, then passed it back. "You've got enough here to make the basis of a paper. I suggest you write it up when all this military distraction is over. Very little of Aleutian geology is known at this time."

Pangs! I had gotten my degree ten years before. I loved geology but graduated at the tail end of the Great Depression which produced no geological employment for me. I drifted into commercial photography. That, too, was interesting. I enjoyed the surprise of each new assignment, the challenge, and the fact that each assignment came finally to an end. Finished! A sense of accomplishment, and on to the next. All that was fine, up to the day I saw a large billboard carrying the result of my biggest and best job, out there for all the passing motorists to see. It gave me a wrench in the middle. I loath billboards. When the draft came my way I sold off the whole photographic outfit. Mixed feelings, of course, but commercial photography had lost its charm. Geology? How could I return ten years late?

Nevertheless, when the war was over, I went back to the University of Wisconsin Geology Library and started my paper on the geology of Adak. One of my former professors, R. C. "Con" Emmons, came by, recognized me and asked, "What are you doing here?"

After looking over the paper he said, "Why don't you come back to geology? You might be able to use this for your master's thesis." My return to geology was under way.

Bob Sharp was and is a well-known geologist and teacher. *Life Magazine* later listed him as one of the ten best teachers in the U.S. Home base was California Tech. He did try one of the giant clams of Shagak Bay but I believe he cooked it instead of having it on the half shell. Cautious scientist. Although I have not seen Bob again, we have been in fairly close contact ever since that day on Adak.

Tapley's Great Hunt

One evening when we were having early chow at our Adak base, Bob Niss poked his head through the doorway and announced enthusiastically, "Tapley shot down a P-38 with his bow and arrow." Bob's head retreated before the explosion of disbelief and laughter almost shattered the windows. We abandoned supper and piled out in search of truth.

Up in the highland west of town, there indeed was a P-38, nose in the tundra and twin tails in the air. There was also our man, T5g Ernest Tapley, with his trusty bow and arrows. He was looking only slightly guilty. Tap was well known among us as a good shot with this hunting tool of his ancestors. But wing a P-38? The War Department would surely hear of this. We would hate to lose Tap. He was perhaps our best all-around mountain man and would be of little use in some military dungeon. That mightiest of hunters was eager to explain. As he did so, I couldn't help trying to visualize a P-38 mounted over the Tapley fireplace.

Tap had gone on an afternoon ptarmigan hunt. When he reached the open highland he decided to warm up with a few trial shots. After a few minutes of that, on impulse, he sent a winged shaft on a vertical flight toward heaven. As he watched the sky, a P-38 slid into view and burst into flames. Down it came and buried its nose in the tundra while its overheated ammunition box made like 4th of July. Technician, fifth grade Tapley, whose specialty was survival, had of course removed himself from the landing site before the landing and assumed the prone position behind a big hummock, safe from the barrage. He now emerged just in time to watch an enraged gentleman riding a parachute make an ungraceful landing near the plane. The gentleman got all tangled up in the ropes and rolled around in the wet grass and mud, which only doubled his rage.

Tapley, still nonplussed by this explosive interference into a peaceful hunt, and slightly disturbed by the coincidence of arrow and aircraft, now rushed to help the entangled pilot. He freed him and got him to his feet. Meanwhile that gentleman unloaded a heartfelt message to his maker and the universe at large. Before the tirade ended, Tap had folded the parachute for him.

Surprisingly soon, a clutch of army vehicles came bouncing up the tundra slope. Men poured out, scooped up pilot and parachute, jumped back into the jeeps and bounced down the slope toward town.

They had not even looked at Tap and no one thanked him for his help. In response, Tap cast off any remnant of guilt and replaced it with pleasure and pride in the quality of his bowmanship.

The next day the pilot's report indicated that while he was on approach to the landing strip, the left engine inexplicably burst into flames. The pilot barely had time to bail out. There was no mention of Tapley or of any arrow embedded in the bowels of the P-38. Military cover-up, probably.

Yakak

My geological notebook was getting fat, and the urge was growing to see those corners of Adak we had not

Over Kagalaska Strait

yet visited. Especially there was Cape Yakak, the southernmost point on Adak, about thirty map miles southwest of town. The cape is the tip of a pancake-like peninsula, almost separated from the main island by the deep V-shaped Bay of Waterfalls. (That name alone caused me to lean perceptibly toward the southwest.) The round-trip cross-country hike would require six days and that would take special arrangements with the colonel. My chance came more suddenly and easily than I could have anticipated.

Jim Ford was now back with us from OQMG to disburse the new Jo-cloth uniforms to the training staff Jim wanted to test his uniform on an extended hike to the tiny radio outpost on Yakak where a small group of men maintained around the clock alert for signs of the enemy. Ever since Pearl Harbor, such outposts were making a habit of staying alert in spite of prolonged boredom and loneliness. How were they equipped? How were they doing? Jim discovered that once a week a small steamer took mail and supplies out to Yakak and that the captain would be glad to take Jim and make arrangements for the visit. Jim requested my company from Colonel Forrest and we were off. The schedule would be one day over by ship and a three-day return hike.

The steamer, about the size of a harbor tugboat, took the sheltered southern route around Adak. While we were threading our way carefully through the narrow channel of Kagalaska Strait, two P-40s in close tandem roared by us executing simultaneous slow rolls just above the water, followed by a burst from the leader's machine gun that kicked up spray around some floating object. Then they were gone. We saw a few whale spouts, a pod of sea lions and some enthusiastic puffins fanning the air before we finally dropped anchor in a tiny sheltered cove on the east side of Cape Yakak. Evening colors were illuminating the tussocks of last year's grass that covered the rolling plateau above the black, vertical rocky cliffs bordering the whole peninsula.

On the cobblestone beach, four men in fatigues were eagerly waiting as the little gas-powered dinghy brought the stern line of the steamer up to the dock. There they all pulled while the captain slacked off the anchor line until the stern of the steamer lay against the dock. There was a good deal of laughter and banter going on as the cargo was unloaded and stacked into a waiting jeep. Outgoing mail and reports were passed onto the steamer which was then hauled out into deeper water for the night. The captain and his one-man crew stayed aboard while the rest of us walked up the jeep trail to the little cluster of buildings that housed the staff and their radio station.

The resident population of this village was six. As we walked up the trail there was considerable horseplay going on among the natives. They kept trying to trip each other which was accented by loud cheers when anyone went down. When the mail was distributed there was more horseplay. One of the men got hold of another's letter. While three others restrained the rightful owner the thief slowly and elaborately opened the pink envelope and sniffed it deeply for perfume, gave a huge sigh, and wiped his eyes. Then he passed it on to the others to sample until the fuming owner was finally allowed to have it.

Then came the ration boxes and another strange ritual. The men opened all the boxes as fast as possible, removed the fruit bars in each and threw them hard at one of their number who caught, ducked, was often hit, but finally retrieved all the bars, stuffed them into a sack, and disappeared over the hill. The men looked at the two mystified guests and roared with laughter. "You'll find out soon enough," we were told.

Jim and I were assigned to the C.O.'s cabin for the night. We had our sleeping bags and the C.O. had a couple of folding army cots. It was pretty much a one-room cabin, spick, span, and tidy. It had a table and a few chairs, a desk, typewriter, file drawers and well-loaded book shelves on one side. On the opposite side were bunks and clothing racks. In between was a wall on which were hung pictures of wife and kids, an M-1 rifle and cartridge belt, and a bow and quiver of arrows. Of special note was a blue fox pelt pinned to the wall by a couple of deeply embedded arrows.

While we waited for the evening meal, our host plied us with small cups of brandy and questions about NPCS which were interwoven with Jim's questions about life on this outpost. I had become fascinated by a peculiar ball game going on outside.

Visibility through the small window was limited and getting poorer in the fading light of evening. The game seemed very vigorous with lots of body contact, bellowing and laughter, but was almost impossible to describe.

It looked like a version of softball. With only four playing, it was every man for himself. The bat was a weathered two by four with a minimum of shaping. The ball looked very light, like a sphere of cork, perhaps a Japanese net float. The bases, if any, were invisible among the hummocks. On one hit, the batter sent the ball straight up where the wind carried it to the rear. The catcher sprinted after it, caught it and continued to run in that direction while the others chased him. In a couple of hundred yards he was tackled, downed and flattened under the pile of bodies.

On another hit the batter swatted the ball into the wind. As he ran for first base, he caught the ball himself and then strolled around the bases while the others stood and watched. He claimed a home run but was ruled out by the others because, in catching the fly, he had put himself out.

Still another hit was caught by the pitcher, relayed much too slowly to the first baseman who then broke and ran like mad with the ball, dived into the outhouse, slammed the door, and locked it in the faces of his pursuers. They banged, yelled, and shook the building. Finally they gave up and let the winner (?) out. The game was called on account of darkness.

"What in the devil is going on out there?" I asked the C.O. He glanced out and said, "Oh, that's the daily physical fitness workout. They call the game 'Bazel-Bawzel'. By the way, how did you like the brandy?" It had been many months since I'd had a taste of hard liquor and it seemed to me like nectar and ambrosia. "One of our guys makes this out of fruit bars. He experimented for a while and then hooked us with a taste. He said he'd be glad to make it for the gang under three conditions. First, we would supply him with the fruit bars. Second, we would not pester him with questions. Third, none of us would enter his work place or reveal it to outsiders. So, since we all enjoy the product we don't really know where he works or what he does."

"Tastes fine to me," said Jim. "I don't have to know everything."

"I see you're an archer," I said. "Did you kill that fox with bow and arrow?" "Oh, no. I won that off one of the guys in a crap game. But I do enjoy using a bow and arrow, except it's too windy most of the time." He took the bow down off the wall, strung it and casually nocked an arrow. "Of course in here there's not much wind. See that round spot on the front door?" With that he made a swift draw and loosed the arrow. It went right through as though the door were a sheet of paper. Jim's usually imperturbable eyebrows went up and my jaw dropped. We had no time to speak. The door opened and in came one of the men carrying supper. He gave the C.O. a sober accusing look and said, "You oughta be more careful." The C.O. said, "Oh, stop your bitchin!" Both Jim and I were still in a state of shock when the archer and the cook collapsed in laughter and pounded each other on the shoulder.

As we rolled in for the night I had the distinct feeling of something strange running around loose in this small group of men. Should we fear for our lives or just relax and enjoy it?

The hike back to Adak Base was highlighted the first day by a visit to a sea lion rookery on the west coast. Long before we got there the aroma of dead fish on the wind alerted us to their presence. There must have been about fifty, mainly big bulls and cows. Most were sunning themselves on a smooth rock shelf that sloped gently down into the sea. A few were in transit in or

Albino sea lion near Yakak

out of the water. When they saw us peeking over the cliff above, there was a burst of roaring and stirring around, but they showed no signs of leaving. On our part, we were not about to move any further into that gag-trigger atmosphere. One of the sea lions was creamy white, reminding me again of Kipling's story of the white seal.

As evening came on, so did the rain. Jim Ford got out his carbine and harvested a ptarmigan while I pitched our tent near one of innumerable small shallow lakes that decorate this plateau. That night supper consisted mainly of boiled ptarmigan and ptarmigan broth.

"What do you make of that radio gang?" I asked him. He smiled. "A bit weird, eh? I think they said they had been on this job for a couple of years. Kinda long for such a small gang to be isolated and confined under such rugged conditions and lack of action. The fact that the cabins are clean and in good repair, the fact that the men are all still there, running an important operation with a sense of responsibility and pride, no one in a straight jacket in spite of what could be a completely boring and lonely existence—well, even though there seems to be a certain wackiness that occasionally gets rough and risky, the gang looked surprisingly sound to me."

"Go a little farther," I said. "Do you think the wackiness is a step toward degeneration or do you think it serves some useful purpose for them?"

"Hmm," said Jim, "as the C.O. said, it seems to serve for physical fitness. Beyond that I suppose it may help block other more disastrous mental escape routes."

"Well," I said, "I was thinking of what Bob Niss said about the ravens and their crazy antics that some times border on the lethal. Bob said, 'it's the way anyone gets if he stays in the Aleutians long enough.' I kinda like the idea that there are times in the lives of men and ravens when wackiness has survival value."

Trial by Rockfall II

Was it spring fever or some other mood that affected me when our fourth class arrived on June 1? This time there were only forty candidates. Was the Alaskan Department getting to the bottom of the barrel or was the task force getting up to strength? The instructional period was again two months, pretty short to build a savvy mountain soldier. Did that make any difference or was the training of less importance?

Rock climbing on the Palisades.
Kuluk Bay background

It seemed possible that a collapsing Germany and the increasing momentum and success of the war against Japan was carrying a signal, official or ephemeral, that the Kuril Task Force was creeping toward the back burner.

These questions and feelings were mine only. The thirteen officers and twenty-seven enlisted men of Class 4 were gung ho. Very shortly we were all working hard again. Up ahead was a new and moderately dangerous exercise we wished to try, but the men had to be in top shape if it was to work.

Well known to mountaineers is the fact that spring is the time of highest hazard from rockfall. This is especially true of the Aleutians with their prolonged period of diurnal freeze-thaw that shatters the rock, loosens the fragments and moves them outward on a cliff face where they poise, ready to fall spontaneously, whenever the sun frees them from bondage.

That characteristic of the cliff face of the Palisades attracted our attention as a spectacular place for advanced rappelling but later engaged our thoughts as an untested opportunity for military strategy. The heavy surf that characteristically bashes the Aleutian Islands makes certain that much of the island shorelines are cliff faces. In terms of our combat assignment, we had plenty of evidence that the same was true for the Kurils. It seemed probable that our enemy would not spend too much time or resources on defense development of the cliffs. Most cliffs are faced with shattered and rotten volcanic rubble, death traps to those who try to climb them with the techniques of that day.

Unlike most of the Aleutian cliffs, the Palisades are composed of a dense tough volcanic rock called columnar basalt (because of a joint pattern that forms vertical columns and hence vertical cliffs), technically difficult to climb but not nearly as treacherous as the rubble cliffs. Columnar basalt cliffs are not uncommon in the Aleutians and, under the right conditions, might favor surprise for an enemy who did not distinguish among different cliff types. The right conditions would include the kinds of vertical cracks for which there were climbing techniques even in that day. The swarm of people now scaling the sheer faces and overhangs of El Capitan and Half-Dome in Yosemite Valley tell us that what you can climb depends on what you know. As with Goretex and bazookas, we didn't have all that knowledge in the spring of 1945 but we had a little and were searching for more.

Not until late May or June did we dare start probing the face of Palisades. Memory of the terrible fall on Mt. Moffet was still strongly with us. A fall on Palisades would probably mean a

Rapelling off Palisades

couple of long bounces and then the icy water of Kuluk Bay where an uninjured man might last ten minutes. As the team explored, we exposed only two climbers at a time. They were always on belay from above and far enough apart so that a rock fall from one would not affect the other. Once in a while one would deliberately kick off some loose rock and watch the face closely for signs of larger movement. Where vegetation did cover the face, we even shoveled through it in a few places to check the soundness of the rock beneath.

What we found was encouraging. The rock seemed generally sound and in a number of places the vertical columns had broken off cleanly at right angles, leaving broad steps useful both in climbing and rappelling. In many areas of the face, crack climbing, though possible, was not necessary. In the end we located and marked several routes that looked safe for the ascent of our best students under close guidance by the staff. And finally there was an unanticipated bonus. Wave action at the base of the cliff had cut out a narrow shelf or notch a few feet above sea level. It could be used for easy landing from a small boat and for rapid lateral movement of troops along the cliff.

One weekend when no one else was on the face, Jim Ford and I rappelled down the cliff to the wave-cut notch and started to explore it for extent and consistency. Jim was a persistent learner and a good mountaineer. He was also good company under any circumstance. Above the perpetual bashing and rumble of wave and wind I thought I heard a voice. We stopped to listen. There it was again, directly above us on the cliff. Damn! No one was supposed to be there this afternoon. We were in a thoroughly risky position and quickly turned around to get out of there as fast as possible.

It was too late. We heard a barrage of shouts and a grinding crunch as a substantial block of the cliff broke loose. I looked up in time to see an explosion of rock fragments, big and small, take to the air directly above us. There were too many coming at us all at once to try to dodge individuals. I yelled at Jim to flatten against the cliff face. At that moment I was doing my best to imitate a thin coat of paint on the rock, praying that the combination of helmet and boulder trajectory would be enough. But just in case, I threw my arms over the top of the helmet. In that same split second I felt Jim's long body flatten itself against my back. A winged thought went by too fast to record. "Is he nuts? In that position he will stick out twice as far as he needs to?" Even with my face buried in the columnar basalt I could hear the typical music of a covey of rocks on the wing. Whistles, whispers, howls, flutters, sizzles, screams, ripping and tearing noises punctuated by occasional thuds as they went by, bouncing and sailing and finally splashing into the sea. I even felt the wind from a couple of close ones. But once again luck was with us.

Not so up above. After I'd unloaded a bushel of abusive language on the guilty but invisible party somewhere up on the face, I caught the message that Bob Niss, our master sergeant, had been clobbered on the head by a large chunk. Instantly I was on my way up the cliff via one of our marked routes. Bob's helmet saved his life but he was in a coma. Then he came out of his coma and started to climb toward the rim saying that he was okay and didn't need any help from the likes of us. Then he went back into a coma and fell. He would have followed the rocks had not Tapley, acting with the speed of light, jammed one hand into a crack, grabbed Bob by his belt with the other and pulled him back out of the sky. Then Bob became belligerent and it took four or five guys to hold him down. Then he started laughing and passed out again.

By the time I arrived at the narrow pocket where the gang was located they were wrestling with a powerful and stubborn Bob Niss. When Bob saw me, he busted out laughing and reported how the stupid mob was abusing him and would I please order them off his carcass so he could go home. With help from another group that had gathered at the top of the cliff, we straight-jacketed Bob, hauled him to safety and got him to the hospital. The next morning, except for an aching (but not cracked) head, and a stiff (but not broken) neck Bob was himself again. He listened amazed and unbelieving as we told him of his adventure.

In my concern to get up to the wrestling match on the cliff I had forgotten Jim Ford. Always calm and resourceful, Jim had returned to the rappel ropes and made his way back to the top of the cliff by himself. For a couple more days we had his company. Then he left for OQMG, his mission with us completed.

Near misses like that rockfall tend to return in my dreams from time to time. About a week after Jim left, my night brain replayed the adventure for me. When I woke with the usual jerk and yell I discovered that I had a tentative answer to the question that had zipped by while the rocks were lifting off. Why did Jim leave all that good shelter against the cliff and double his own danger by plastering himself over my back? All at once I felt humble. He was protecting me with his own body. But, damn it, he moved on instinct. There was no time for altruistic thoughts. Right. Like Tapley he had done his thinking in advance, again and again over the course of his life. He was now coded. No need to spend precious time in thought.

A few years after the war was over I was in New York City and took the opportunity and my family to visit the Museum of Natural History, where Jim had an office. He was there. So I took the whole family to meet a special guy. (They had already heard about the rockfall too many times.) We visited, recalled the rock fall and, belatedly, I thanked him.

ZAP!

It's hard for me to remember Class 4. The record shows they did well. Of the forty, twenty-seven became graduates, eight were satisfactory, and five failed or left early.

While they were with us, Lieutenant Colonel Forrest took post commanders on tours to see our men in action and to orient them to the curriculum. A photo record was made, and in other ways we were getting signals that our secrecy was gone and the game was about over.

You can share our surprise when a little over a week after Class 4 disappeared, Class 5 arrived, twelve officers and twenty-seven enlisted men—thirty-nine in all. They were black men who had been gathered from all up and down the Aleutian Islands. It was an experimental class. Most of the group had had an eighth grade education. Some had gone through high school. Two were illiterate and ultimately failed, but they requested to stay with the school anyway because they felt they were learning things of value. None had much experience with the out of doors and even less with mountains. To bring them up to the level of the other classes would probably take a year. How long was this damn war going to last? Best we get started.

August had good weather. We started taking hikes in the foothills to get past the first stiffness that comes from walking on soggy hummocks instead of on boardwalks. The new candidates were in good spirits and good physical condition, so with extra caution we introduced them to mountains. They were not clumsy. Things were looking brighter, and they seemed to be enjoying the exhilaration of high places. Occasionally one would get scared on a steep pitch. Then we would have to pry his fingers off the vegetation, talk him out of his uphill lean toward Mother Earth and coax him back to a vertical stance by pointing out that, tied as he was with a rope, he couldn't fall even if he wanted to.

There was an interesting temperamental contrast between this class and the others. When a member of Class 5 sustained a deep fright or a bruise resulting from clumsiness, he often giggled or laughed and was joined by his buddies. It sounded more like a nervous or fatalistic reaction rather than a matter of humor. But it did appear to reduce tension and to speed the return to calm and steadiness. Beyond that it favored buoyancy and enjoyment of the outing. A similar situation in the other classes had more often elicited a roar of anger, a blast of four-letter words or a gritting silent fury as from an unforgivable insult. Amusingly, had this new group been our only class, Bitchin' Ridge would never have acquired that name. After we had taken Class 5 for its first taste of that ridge, the uninvolved portion of teaching staff, waiting below in camp, asked us on our return, "What was all so damn funny up there? You guys sounded as though you were watching Laurel and Hardy."

Before we had a chance to take Class 5 on the famous night patrol along the crest of Bitchin' Ridge, America had dropped two unbelievably destructive bombs on Japan and the curtain fell on World War II. A million voices whispered "Thank God." Mine was one of them. The world is still shuddering from the gruesome results.

Spring moon on Adak airport

Fleet returns to Kuluk Bay three days after V-J Day

L'Envoi

Of course a world war doesn't end on the instant. At this point we were in the middle of training Class 5. Our C.O. was away on a temporary assignment. As adjutant, I was suddenly uncertain of what should be done. We let the training continue under its own momentum for a few days. No message from H.Q. came, so I took the liberty of dropping in on the base commander with, "Sir, since the war is over, I wonder if there might be some more useful function for NPCS and our current class in training?" He gave me a chilly look and said, "What are you doing now?" I gave him a thumbnail sketch. Then he asked, "Have you received any orders to change things?" (No, Sir.) "Then I suggest you continue as directed until you do." (Yes, Sir! Snappy salute, about face, and out the door.)

Thus it came about that one whole month after V-J Day, NPCS was still secretly training men for a task force to enter the Kurils. Not quite. After a few days of silliness, we forgot the base commander and bent the assignment into training men for future outdoor recreation in mountain country. It also included (for those who wished) a short course in geology and the geological history of Adak. The new training program succeeded so well that we advertised it in the local weekly and got a half dozen additions to the class.

Finally came the orders that ended our assignment in the Aleutians and dissolved NPCS at the tender age of one and a half years. In that period NPCS, with four instructors and eleven guides, had processed a total of 230 candidates, seventy-nine of whom were deemed good enough to become instructors in the art of survival, mobility and tactics in wet, cold mountain areas.

Tundarena

ADD SUNDAY

VOL VII Number 85 SUNDAY 23 SEPT 1945

NPCS after VJ day

TOUCH FOOTBALL

Friday night's meeting at the Tundarena produced a Touch Football League of 10 teams, and it was announced yesterday that play will begin next Sunday, on the field across from the Tundarena.

The games will be pretty fast--10 [illegible] quarters--and there will probably be 5 games each Sunday afternoon.

This will be 9-man touch. Only a few of the rules differ from the regular football regulations: there must be 5 men in the line on offense; all 5 are eligible to receive passes; and the offensive team must make a touchdown in 4 downs or lose the ball.

We'll carry a list of teams next Sunday.

BASKETBALL GETS GOING

Competition is set to start in the Post Basketball League October 14, and teams may enter the League and make reservations for practice as of today.

Teams organized are supposed to be representative of outfits on company strength level; smaller detachments may combine if they wish. To enter the League, submit by letter the organization name and the number of team entries. A final player roster need not be submitted until the end of the first half of the basketball season.

All entries must be in by October 3. Address them to the Post Athletic Officer, Tundarena.

A school for BB officials will start Oct. 1. Qualified officials may work league games at $1 per game.

How To Be An Outdoor Man

Starting a week from tomorrow, October 1, the North Pacific Combat School will conduct a voluntary, non-military course in the theory and practice of the more rugged aspects of outdoor living.

The object of the course, depending entirely on the individual's purpose in taking it, is to provide useful training for anybody who intends to spend a lot of time outdoors, as either business or pleasure--for, in other words, future amateur or professional mountain climbers, guides, hunters, rangers, explorers, etc.

The course will last 3 weeks (another one may start October 29). It's being offered to personnel from the entire Chain, so the quota for this island is small --12 men. Both EM and officers are eligible. Qualifications are listed as including an interest in the subject, "excellent physical condition," above-average intelligence and an excellent record in the applicant's organization. Application may be made through your unit commander.

Attendance is, of course, voluntary. It is further guaranteed that your enrolling will in no circumstances delay your return to the US, if your number comes up.

The course will include some theory--something about how mountains have affected man, and a little of the natural science ~~(geology, botany, climatology)~~ involved in mountain life--but most of it will be practical instruction and activity. Some categories: survival in the mountains; clothing--how to choose it and take care of it; special mountaineering techniques; camping and cooking; emergency foods--where to find them and how to fix them; land navigation; and bushcraft. There will also be some practice in firing weapons at unknown ranges in rough country.

Clipping from The Adakian, *"How To Be An Outdoor Man," Vol. VII, no. 85, Sunday, September 23, 1945*

In spite of all the seeming changes to our mission, this core assignment was always there. A new cadre of seventy-nine instructors doesn't look too bad. It was their luck that, like the extra boxes of ammunition, they were not needed for this war.

By this time, our NPCS instructional team was a well-knit bunch whose members thoroughly enjoyed each other. The thought of it ending suddenly, breaking up into individuals, each flying off in a different direction, was a shock. Most of us had been in the army so long that our former life had faded into an almost unreal distant past that had little connection with the present. Now here we were getting ready to plunge back into that mysterious foreign land of the civilian, where we could no longer lean on each other. Would we ever see each other again? What would we be doing next year? Where would we be? What civilian work would we be fit for?

In the middle of all that visceral turmoil, one overpowering drive superseded all others and guided the action for most of us. Home! Gotta get home! Each of us had a mimeograph sheet with the names and addresses of all members of NPCS. That was comforting. What we didn't sense then was that in a couple of years that sheet would be almost useless. Many of those addresses were parental, or in any case little more than a short-lived springboard. Also the parents themselves were approaching retirement and were beginning to move.

We packed our gear and waited our turns for transportation home. NPCS broke up, one or two chunks at a time. There was lots of pounding shoulders, waving, yelling insults, and good wishes. Also there were unseen lumps in the throat and awareness of an unforgettable adventure ending.

Epilogue

Adak Base was in a state of happy chaos as we all tried to bring the huge combat machine to a halt and get things turned around and rolling east. Individual pressures toward home added up to a powerful but not always orderly force. I found myself slowly creeping forward, moving from one long line of soldiers to another, but I was concentrating on my own chores. It took a few shocks before I started taking a broader look at the big parade. One long line finally led me into the presence of the supply officer where I turned in a rucksack filled with items issued to me over the years. When I came to the little one-burner stove that had cooked my camp meals for the last four years with nary a failure, I asked the officer if I could buy it or arrange to keep it. "Oh, no. All issued items must be returned. I'd probably get court martialed if I let you keep it." So I handed it to him. He looked at its aged and somewhat battered condition, shrugged his shoulders and tossed it into a trash can. If he was throwing it away, why not toss it to me? He stared at me in icy defiance. A hot spark of anger glowed in my gizzard as I walked out.

A few hundred feet down the boardwalk and off to one side was a smoldering trash fire. A pile of unused sleeping bags were being cremated. The acrid scent of scorched goose down harmonized well with my rising fury. "Why in all hell are you burning these new sleeping bags?" I asked the lad tending the fire. He jumped when he saw my captain's bars but answered the best he could, "I was ordered to, sir." I cooled down and asked him if he had been given any reason. "Well, sir, they said something about not being able to take the bags back to the states because transportation was too expensive and it would wreck the economy and stuff." Obviously that was ridiculous. The young guy must have garbled the message, so I told him to carry on and left with the uproar increasing in my midsection.

All over Adak Base fires were burning up the leftovers from the campaign, much of it in still unopened cartons. Out in Kuluk Bay heavier unburnables such as weapons and machine parts were pushed overboard to decorate the bottom of that fiord. One of my 10th Mountain gang told me he had watched unopened cartons of the little camp stoves being loaded on a barge to be dumped in the bay.

The worst of all was the giant lumberyard. It took most of two weeks to burn it up, but with the help of bulldozers working night and day, it was finally obliterated from an island that had never known a tree. I thought of the Aleuts who might well return to Adak. They would have cherished the supply and used it well.

And the young man burning the sleeping bags had *not* garbled the explanation given him. Again and again I heard the same justification for the unjustifiable wastage of resources and labor. Oh, we can't take all this back (or sell it to the soldiers, or give it to the poor, or leave it for the Aleuts, etc.); it would upset the economy. I am no economist, but if this is a fact, there is a monstrous flaw in the economy that should be corrected before we have completely blasted America the Beautiful.

It was October 15 when, "Hey! Close your footlocker, pick up your new orders, sign out and meet me at the air strip in two hours. Me and you are going home!" Capt. Harry Hitchcock charged back out the door to take care of his own paperwork. Going home! If there was a sudden knot in my throat at least it didn't interfere with my race through the routine obstacle course for departure. That was achieved in record time with military skill and bearing, including the sheet attesting to my completion of duty signed by Marty Krause, now a major and acting in the absence of Colonel Forrest. Marty gave me a sour look as we shook hands. He would have to stay on until the last NPCS man was gone. Going home! Sometimes I had wondered if it would ever happen.

Harry was a wheeler-dealer. He had accidentally encountered the Canadian air vice marshall downtown and learned that he was passing through Adak in his private bomber en route to Vancouver. A couple of drinks followed by a couple of well-aimed questions and Harry had wangled a lift for both of us. The air vice marshall was a stocky, pleasant bundle of vigor with piercing blue eyes and a warm smile. Clearly he enjoyed the chance to help boost a couple of homesick soldiers toward their respective medicine lodges. "Welcome aboard my magic carpet," he said, showing us into the passenger area. Bomber, eh? Well, it might have started as a bomber. We were in what looked more like a well-appointed drawing room complete with table, desk, book racks, comfortable chairs, a divan, carpet and, would you believe, a picture window set low in the fuselage so one could look down on the world without leaving his chair. The chairs were bolted-down swivel affairs equipped with safety belts. Something about this luxurious flying office made me think of Captain Nemo and his fantastic submarine *Nautilus*.

Pilot, copilot, navigator were in the last stages of their check list. Vice Marshall Nemo joined us in the drawing room and we all fastened seat belts. The room was well insulated from the roar of the twin engines, but a gentle vibration told us the props were turning. From the window we got a good moving panorama of Adak Base as the plane slowly pivoted around at the end of the runway. In order: Mt. Moffet, NPCS HQ, the Palisades, Kuluk Bay and beyond it Great Sitkin and its vapor plume. Strange internal tugging. Would I ever see them again? Then, with a long thunderous rumble we lifted off. Adak and Great Sitkin slipped by below and behind and were gone.

In all the excitement of the hasty departure I had only glanced carelessly at my new orders. I was going home, wasn't I? What else did I need to know? Sitting in the Vice Marshall's drawing room, surrounded by blue sky and puffy clouds, I now pulled the orders out for a closer look. True, I was going home but it seems there were to be some detours. The key lines in the order that I had missed said, "...relieved from duty with the Alaskan Dept. and assigned to the Office of Quartermaster General, Washington, D.C." What had I done to deserve such torture? The location suggested the crafty hand of Jim Ford or Maj. Bob Bates. Maynie and Charlie Jr. were living with her parents in New York City at that time. Perhaps by manipulative bumbling, the unreliable postwar transportation might force me to go through New York en route to D.C. I felt better for that thought.

Mt. Makushin with its plume and the little bay within a bay that marked Dutch Harbor were sliding by below when I got back to the window. We were about half way to Anchorage where we would have supper and spend the night. The pilot discarded some altitude, bringing the ship down almost to ground level when we came over the outer point of the Alaska Peninsula. As the tundra streamed by, we caught glimpses of Alaskan grizzly bears charging across country to escape the plane. Then, after a year and a half of tundra, we began to see trees again. If it had been possible I would certainly have joined the hug-a-tree gang. Trees marked the outer edge of home.

The next morning we lifted off from Anchorage in a thick fog. For about half an hour in a welter of fierce up and downdrafts we played a scary game of cat and mouse with the rocky outcrops and spires of the Chugach Mountains. In one case, with the plane at full throttle and maximum climbing angle, we lost a thousand feet of altitude in half a minute. For that half minute we were almost weightless. Once in a while a small rent in the curtain of fog gave us a split-second glimpse of a snow-splashed rock face none too far away. With the plane pitching and rolling, we couldn't be sure whether we were looking up or down. Finally we cleared the crests. The runaway elevator ride was over. All of us, pilots included, could breathe normally again.

The vice marshall, though headed for Vancouver, was scheduled to make a two-day inspection stop at Queen Charlotte Islands. Our unbelievable host had made arrangements by radio for a couple of his young pilots to fly Harry and me in a small airplane to Seattle just to keep us moving toward home. He waved us off with a huge grin on his face. After signing in to United States at Seattle Port of Embarkation, Harry and I parted, each to take whatever transport was available.

I digress here to recount an event that still haunts me. Harry and I maintained contact through the years. Once in the 1980s he dropped in to see me in my present home. Then there was a period of several years of lost contact. One night at 2:00 A.M. the phone rang. I answered.

"This is Charles Bradley speaking." There was some scrabbling at the other end of the line. Then, "Ah—hugh—*who's* speaking?"

"Charles Bradley," I said.

Then, "Oh—Charlie, it's you. I was rooting around in my pockets and found a scrap of paper with this telephone number on it so I decided to call and see who it was."

"Hey" said I, "It's 2 A.M.—who the devil am I talking to?"

"Oh—uh—this is Harry Hitchcock." He sounded strange, disconnected, drunk maybe. "Sorry to bother you."

"For goodness sake, Harry, what are you doing at this time of night?"

"Me? oh—well—I'm dying."

I was stunned. No he didn't sound drunk. "Harry, where are you? I asked sharply.

"Right here in this telephone booth."

"Where's that?"

"Don't know. Doesn't make any difference though."

"Is anyone with you?"

"Nope, Charlie, they're all gone. I don't know anyone any more."

"But, Harry, surely I can call some one to give you some help."

"Don't bother. It won't help. I'm dying. Bye, Charlie." Click!

Desperately I rang the operator and she did her best to find the connection but it was too late.

In Seattle, planes, trains and busses were overrun with soldiers. The only good thing was that military personnel had priority over civilians. I got a train ticket that ended in Chicago where I had to enter another long line and continue to fight my way toward our nation's capital. Finally I got another ticket, and guess what, it ended in New York City. Furthermore the train departed three days hence, which gave me a chance to run up to Madison and see my parents. Three days later I was on the slowest, dullest, most inefficient and exasperating train I've ever taken in my life. It finally came to rest at Grand Central Station. With heart pounding my ribs to pulp, I stepped off. And there she was.

It took a lot of hugging to make up for those two years. We couldn't do it all that afternoon but we made a good start. After a while Maynie asked, "Aren't you going to greet your son?" I jumped with guilt and looked around. There was a mob of people on the platform, many of whom were kids running around and yelling, but none of them looked familiar. Maynie pointed to a quiet, serious, blond youngster a few feet away. He was very busy cleaning the marble staircase with the seat of his britches. He saw me watching him and paused to give me a short, sharp but disinterested glance and returned to his stair-cleaning assignment. It was then I began to realize that friendship with my son was by no means a foregone relationship. It did not even exist yet. Worse, he not only did not recognize me as his father but knew for a fact that I was *not* "Daddy." Maynie, embarrassed and nonplussed stubbornly insisted that I *was* Daddy. Just as stubbornly Charlie Jr. said "No!"—one of his few words and one well used, I discovered later.

In a movie, this moment of revelation that I was not "Daddy" would have been very embarrassing to Mom and very sinister to Pop. As it turned out, there was no family crisis in the making, only general puzzlement. On the way to the house on East 90th, Maynie drove so that young Charlie could sit on my lap. He didn't want to sit on my lap. He seemed surprised and a little annoyed at my continuing presence and my blotting up his mother's time. So he kept his distance, playing in the back seat, and I took the additional opportunity to blot up some more of his mother's time.

Charlie's verbal vocabulary was not very great yet but he was exceptionally eloquent at body language. After we were settled in the house, Charlie moved swiftly to clear up one mystery and demonstrate his knowledge of logic without words. Indicating that we were to follow, he climbed the stairs rapidly on all fours and crawled to the bathroom, pulled himself upright on the leg of the wash basin and said. "uuh—uuh" to get our undivided attention. Then he pointed to Maynie's folding alarm clock and said, "Daddy." He was right. For the last two years Maynie had pointed toward a photograph mounted in the clock and said, "Daddy." He had learned it well and could even say it.

Clearly the problem of my paternal relationship with my son was going to be more difficult than any of the three of us could have imagined.

Out of the cosmos I snitched a couple of golden days with Maynie and the still suspicious Charlie Jr. Then I was off to D.C. and my last assignment, something with the Research and Development Branch of OQMG. The train to D.C. was bulging with passengers. I was assigned a couple of square feet in the area between cars where I could stand and bounce around and cuss for six hours and nobody could hear me above the uproar of cars banging on each other. The space was well air conditioned with free-flowing late November air. There was no danger of my falling because there was no space to fall into. Five other soldiers supported me in a manner to which I have never become accustomed. The late November air I was accustomed to. The roar and banging was no worse than a williwaw but the intimate contact with a maximum number of human bodies in minimum space was new and not to be cherished. When the six hour ordeal was up and someone opened the door we erupted out on the platform and were off and running in all directions.

My direction ultimately took me to a desk in OQMG occupied by Maj. Robert Bates, well-known mountaineer and, in the 10th Mountain circles, equally well known as the man who saw to it that America's first mountain combat division was properly supplied with the very special gear needed to conduct that kind of combat. Bob and the others associated with that supply job had started from scratch. It's hard for me to visualize the network of trails, defining the specific needs, designing an item, fabricating it, testing it, modifying and testing it again and finally mass producing it for the division to test before taking it into combat, and all this for hundreds of special items. But that is the kind of operation America does well—especially with the help of people like Bob.

Bob looked up and smiled as I walked in. Now I would find out why I was here. Actually it wasn't too complicated. It seems there was a wad of loose ends regarding the special gear for Aleutian soldiers. OQMG needed to standardize a list for future reference and use. NPCS and others had made so many different requests at such high velocity that the quartermaster, in spite of Jim Ford's reports, was unsure of what gear turned out well and what still needed testing.

As a matter of fact I felt pleased that Bob had requested me. Back at Adak I was not at all sure that our tiny NPCS operation had nailed down anything useful or important for future Aleutian operations. So here was an opportunity to help. Bob thought that my assignment should not take more than a couple of months. "A couple of *months*! How about a week?" Bob laughed. Others in the area smiled and chuckled. "Nothing happens very fast here but don't let that observation slow you down. There are lots of people here who can help you and will be glad to. You will have a secretary at your call. But don't underestimate the scrutiny you are going to have, the picky questions, the choices that must be made, the debates you will have to face."

If a seasoned operator like Bob thought it might take two months, might it not take me four? "What are the chances of my finding rental housing for Maynie and Charlie? After two damn years I need some time with them. Charlie doesn't even believe I'm his father. I can't let that go on."

Bob oozed optimism. After a few phone calls he found a nice little house on the other side of the Potomac. In less than a week the Bradleys were at home. During the day I searched for the right ropes to pull at OQMG. In the evening and on weekends I pursued a working relationship with Charlie. Additional obstacles had surfaced that had to be overcome. Charlie was now homesick for Grandma and Grandpa and his life at 61 East 90th, New York. There was no substitute. As diversion we finally came up with a game new to the world. Thus no one played it any better than we did. Best of all Charlie enjoyed it. I record it here in case there are some exhausted fathers out there at wit's end and needing renewal.

On the walls around the living room of our new home were many pictures of animals and birds. With Charlie riding my shoulders, we made the rounds daily while I identified each animal for him. Having learned a lesson from Maynie's alarm clock, I deliberately did not use the standard names of the critters in order to avoid such future difficulties as "cat" identifying exclusively a picture on the wall of a small house in Virginia. Instead I employed my capacity for imitating animal voices. When we stopped at the cat picture I snarled like a cat wading into combat. Charlie would imitate my imitation. Later he would identify the animal without my prompting. He would make the rounds on my shoulder, barking, honking, mooing, quacking, gobbling, snarling and whinnying in the correct order. It brought the house down. Being human, he enjoyed the applause, and I think the exercise helped bring us together in spirit. When we met in the morning there were genuine smiles.

That winter (1945–1946) was one in which Washington, D.C., got more than its standard load of snow. Auto traffic was an impossibly stalled mess. But skiing was not at all bad, especially since there were almost no skiers to interfere. At OQMG I was able to borrow a pair of skis (probably nonstandardized). Then came the real breakthrough. In the office of the curator of winter gear, I saw high on the shelf an unusual backpack. It consisted of shoulder straps that supported an L-shaped frame for carrying boxes. Suddenly I could visualize Charlie sitting lashed on the carrying step while I took him skiing with me. "What's that?" I asked the curator. "Oh, they call that an Everest pack. It was designed for carrying a variety of loads on an Everest expedition." "Where could I get one?" I asked. "You can't," he said. "They don't make them any more." "You don't happen to have another that I could borrow for a day or two to give my son a ski ride?" "No," he said, "but you'll notice my back is turned, I'm hard of hearing and my eyesight is none too good." So that afternoon I went skiing in Virginia with Charlie on my back cheering me on with "Ung! Ung! Ung!" I should add that there never was a pack that served more people with kids for so many years and for two generations.

On February 3, 1946, after five years in the army, I was released from duty. Those last months at OQMG were spent trying to untangle the records and reports, select the best items for standardization or further testing, and nail them down for future troops faced with wet, cold mountain combat. In other words, I was trying to make sure that the lessons learned in NPCS would not all be lost. It was a very satisfying way to end the great adventure. I shook hands with Bob Bates and others in that wonderful team that supported so well our mountain troops of World War II.

I was eager to leave, to start my civilian life again, to start graduate work in geology, to have my own home and some home life. But oddly, now and then I had lingering worries about those future mountain troops. The network of OQMG channels leading to standardization was so complex and confusing, I never could be quite certain that I had finished my assignment correctly. I could almost hear some exasperated major, standing in a horizontal slush storm, roaring, "How in hell can my men fight a war out here when they are wearing water soaked shoes and clothes, trying to sleep in leaky tents that blow away, no way to cook food or dry out. Who's responsible for all this junk?"

Bibliography

Bates, Robert. Letters to author, 1992.

Bergamini, David. *Japan's Imperial Conspiracy*. New York: William Morrow and Company, Inc., 1971.

Bowes, William. Letters to author, 1993.

Bradley, C. "Geological Notes on Adak and the Aleutian Chain." *Amer. Jour. of Sci.* 246 (1948).

———. "Play Behavior in Northern Ravens." *The Passenger Pigeon* 40, no. 4 (1978).

Capps, S. R. "Notes on the Geology of the Alaskan Peninsula and Aleutian Islands." *U.S. Geological Survey* 857 (1934).

Casewit, Curtis W. *Mountain Troopers! The Story of the 10th Mountain Division*. New York: Thomas Y. Crowell Company, 1972.

Cloe, John Haile. *The Air Force in Alaska, Part II: Build-up to Dutch Harbor, June 1940–June 1942*. Elmendorf Air Force Base, Alaska: Office of History, Alaskan Air Command, 1986.

———. *The Aleutian Warriors: A History of the 11th Air Force & Fleet Air Wing 4*, Part 1. Anchorage, Alaska/Missoula, Montana: Anchorage Chapter—Air Force Association and Pictorial Histories Publishing Company, Inc., 1991.

Cohen, Stan. *The Forgotten War, A Pictorial History of World War II in Alaska and Northwestern Canada*, Vol. 3. Missoula, Montana: Pictorial Histories Publishing Company, 1992.

Collins, Henry Bascom. *The Aleutian Islands*. War Background Studies #21 (Washington, D.C.: Smithsonian Institution, 1899).

Conn, Stetson, Rose C. Engelman, and Byron Fairchild. *Guarding the United States and Its Outposts*. Washington, D.C.: Office of the Chief Military History, 1964.

Costello, John. *The Pacific War*. New York: Rawson, Wade Publishers, Inc., 1981.

Denfield, D. Colt. "After the Battle, The Air Raid on Dutch Harbor." *Battle of Britain Prints International* 62 (1988).

Denver Public Library, 10th Mountain Archives

Dod, Karl C. *The Corps of Engineers: The War against Japan*. Washington, D.C.: Office of the Chief of Military History, 1966.

Evans-Goodhue, Cornelia. *Journey into the Fog*. New York: Doubleday Doran, 1944.
Faulkner, Sandra McDermott and Robert L. S. Spude. *Naval Operating Base, Dutch Harbor and Fort Mears, Unalaska Island, Alaska*. Anchorage: National Park Service, Alaska Region, 1987.
Fisher, Raymond H. *Bering's Voyages, Whither & Why*. Seattle: University of Washington Press, 1977.
Ford, Corey. *Where the Sea Breaks its Back*. Boston: Little, Brown & Co., 1966.
Forrest, Frank. Letters to author, 1989–1992.
Garfield, Brian. *The Thousand Mile War. World War II in Alaska and the Aleutians*. New York: Doubleday, 1969; New York: Ballantine Books, 1973.
Greenfield, Kent Roberts, Robert R. Palmer, and Bell I. Wiley. *The Organization of Group Combat Troops, US Army in World War II*. Washington, D.C.: Historical Division, Department of the Army, 1947.
Griggs, R. F. *The Valley of Ten Thousand Smokes*. Washington, D.C.: National Geographic Society, 1942.
Hammett, Dashiell and Robert Colodny. *The Battle of the Aleutians 1942–43 in the Capture of Attu: Tales of World War II in Alaska As Told By the Men Who Fought There*. Anchorage: Alaska Northwest Publishing Company, 1984.
Hunt, William R. *Arctic Passage*. New York: Scribners, 1975.
Jackman, Albert. Letters to author, 1989–1992.
Judson, Sheldon. "Late Glacial and Post Glacial Chronology on Adak." *Journ of Geol* 54 (1946).
Kipling, Rudyard. *The Jungle Book, The White Seal*. New York: Grosset & Dunlap, 1893.
Lee, Ulysses. *The Employment of Negro Troops, US Army in WWII*. Washington, D.C.: Office of the Chief of Military History, 1966.
Mahon, John K. and Romana Danysh. *Infantry: Part I: Regular Army*. Army Lineage Series. Washington, D.C.: Office of the Chief of Military History, 1972.
Matloff, Maurice. *Strategic Planning for Coalition Warfare 1943–1944*. Washington, D.C.: Office of the Chief of Military History, 1959.
Michner, James. *Alaska*. New York: Random House, 1988.
Military Orders to C. Bradley from 201 File 1942–1946.
Morgan, Murray C. *Bridge to Russia*. New York: E. P. Duttan, 1947.
Morison, Samuel Eliot. *Aleutians, Gilberts and Marshalls: June 1942–April 1944*. Boston: Little, Brown and Company, 1990.
Murie, Margaret. Letter to author, 1990.
Murie, Olaus. "Fauna of the Aleutian Islands and Alaskan Peninsula." *U.S. Department of the Interior, Fish and Wildlife Service* 61 (1959).
Oliver, Simeon (Nutchuk). *Son of the Smoky Seas*. Mesner, New York: Self-published, 1941.
Pote, Winston. *Mountain Troops: 10th Mountain Division, Camp Hale, Colorado*. Camden, Maine: Down East Books, 1982.

Quick, Horace. Letters to author, 1990.
Sharp, R. B. "Notes on the Geology of Attu, an Aleutian Island." *Jour of Geol* 56 (1947).
Taber, Richard D. "The Winter Birds of Adak, Alaska." *The Condor* 48 (1946).
Tapley, Ernest. Letters to author, 1991.
Thompson, Erwin. "After the Battle, Attu Forty Years After." *Publisher Battle of Britain Prints International* 62 (1988).
———. Emergency Foods in the Aleutians. Prepared under the direction of the ACS, G-2, ADC. Reproduced by Engineering Section ADC., 1943.
Willett, Hurd C. *Descriptive Meteorology.* New York: Academic Press, Inc., 1944.
Wilson, John B. *Armies, Corps, Divisions, and Separate Brigades.* Army Lineage Series. Washington, D.C. Center of Military History, 1987.
Whymper, Edward. *Scrambles Amongst the Alps*, 6th edition. London, England: John Murray Publisher, 1954.

Index

Charles C. Bradley was born in Chicago in 1911. He received his bachelor's degree, master's, and Ph.D. from the University of Wisconsin, all in geology, in 1935, 1947, and 1950 respectively. He pursued his graduate degrees after his return to civilian life from the 10th Mountain Division, Army of the U.S., with which he served from 1941 to 1944, and the North Pacific Combat School from 1944 to 1946. A professor of geology at both the University of Wisconsin and Montana State University (MSU), he also held the position of dean of the College of Letters and Sciences, MSU, coordinator at the MSU Center for Environmental Studies, and codirector of research at the Leopold Memorial Reserve in Baraboo, Wisconsin. He is a member of several professional societies and his research has been published in numerous scientific journals. He was also a professional photographer. Dr. Bradley continues to combine his interest in the outdoors with research. With his wife, Nina, he works on prairie and savanna restoration from spring to autumn and during the winter, cuts firewood, shovels snow, and skis around the Leopold Reserve, keeping records of animal tracks.